The
Data Lakehouse
Architecture

Bill Inmon

Ranjeet Srivastava

Technics Publications

115 Linda Vista
Sedona, AZ 86336 USA
https://www.TechnicsPub.com

Edited by Jamie Hoberman
Cover design by Lorena Molinari

First Printing 2022

Copyright © 2022 by Bill Inmon and Ranjeet Srivastava

ISBN, print ed.   9781634622783
ISBN, Kindle ed. 9781634622790
ISBN, ePub ed.   9781634622806
ISBN, PDF ed.   9781634622813

Library of Congress Control Number: 2022941420

Dedicated to my family, friends, and well-wishers for all their support.

-   **Ranjeet Srivastava**

Contents

Introduction _____ 1

Chapter 1: The Data Lakehouse Architecture _____ 3
   Types of data in the data lakehouse _____ 3
   Managing data in the data lakehouse _____ 6
   Evolution of the data lakehouse _____ 7
   Analytical infrastructure _____ 8
   Maintaining the data lakehouse _____ 9
   Data lakehouse environment _____ 10

Chapter 2: The Structured Environment _____ 13
   Efficiency of processing _____ 13
   Advent of online systems _____ 17
   Service level agreement _____ 18
   Transactions _____ 19
   Creating transaction systems _____ 24
   Enter the data warehouse _____ 26
   Storing data over time _____ 29

Chapter 3: The Textual Environment _____ 31
   Context _____ 32
   Textual disambiguation _____ 33
   Database structure _____ 38
   Benefits from understanding text _____ 41

Chapter 4: Analog/IoT Data Architecture _____ 43
   Examples _____ 43
   Data characteristics _____ 46
   Analyzing data _____ 50

Making sense of machine-generated data _____ 54
Data capture _____ 56
Data archival _____ 57
Value of data samples _____ 58
Examples _____ 58

Chapter 5: The Data Lakehouse Canonical Model _____ 61
Canonical data model _____ 61
Connectors _____ 62
Individual canonical data models _____ 67
Different strengths of connectivity _____ 68

Chapter 6: Data Warehouse and Data Lakehouse _____ 69
Enter the data warehouse _____ 69
Data mart _____ 71
Data lakehouse _____ 71
Comparing the data warehouse and the data lakehouse _ 73

Chapter 7: Dynamics of Data Lakehouse Processing _____ 77
Data flowing into the data lakehouse _____ 78
Data scientist and the data architect _____ 79
Analytical sandbox _____ 80

Chapter 8: The Data Lakehouse Paradigm _____ 83
Must be requirements-driven _____ 83
When to use what _____ 84
Architectural paradigm _____ 86
Data processing stages _____ 87
Analytical workbench _____ 89

Chapter 9: Data Lakehouse Housekeeping _____ 95
Data integration and interoperability _____ 98

Master references for the data lakehouse _____ *101*

Data lakehouse privacy, confidentiality, and data

    protection _____ *104*

"Data future-proofing™" in a data lakehouse _____ *107*

Five phases of "Data Future-proofing" _____ *113*

Data lakehouse routine maintenance _____ *124*

Chapter 10: FDM in Data Lakehouse _____ **127**

FDM process _____ *127*

Modeling strategy _____ *129*

Design strategy _____ *132*

Implementation strategy _____ *134*

FDM as a business mandate _____ *136*

Chapter 11: Leveraging Data Effectively in the Data Lakehouse 139

Data storage _____ *140*

Cloud versus non-cloud _____ *142*

Microservices _____ *142*

Security _____ *151*

Index _____ **153**

Introduction

First there was structured, transaction-based data. And with structured data came applications. Applications grew and data needed to be shared. Then came extract programs. Extract programs moved data from one application to the next. Soon the applications were a big jumble known as the spider web environment. The spider web environment was a large, unmanageable mess. The discomfort of the spider web environment led to the data warehouse, which provided a solid foundation of data for the corporation. The data warehouse unraveled the complexities of the spider web environment.

Soon text data appeared. There was tremendous value in the data within text. However, structured systems were not using this data. With textual ETL, it became possible to combine structured data for analytics. Textual ETL opened the door to the data found in text.

Then analog/IoT data appeared. A machine produced analog IoT data as part of standard operational processing. Analog/IoT data had very different characteristics and properties than structured or textual data. These profound differences presented many challenges to the data analyst trying to make sense of the data. But there was still business value within analog/IoT data.

The first reaction people had in dealing with these three types of data was to build a data lake. In a data lake, the data was simply copied from its source in the hopes that the data would be useful to an end-user analyst. But people quickly discovered that a data lake was not useful. Data in the data lake was not integrated, documented, or connected. Placing data in a data lake was pointless because no one could use the data. Very soon, the data lake turned into a data swamp.

Out of this morass, came the notion that an analytical infrastructure needed to be placed over the data lake for the data to become useful. Once the analytical infrastructure was in place, the data lake became a data lakehouse.

The analytical infrastructure over the data lake had many important and necessary components:

- Data models
- Taxonomies
- Lineage
- Key resolution
- Inline contextualization mapping
- Encoding resolution

With the data lake and analytical infrastructure built, the end user now had a complete, accessible, and understandable environment for analytical processing.

CHAPTER 1

The Data Lakehouse Architecture

Types of data in the data lakehouse

There are three types of data we use to make decisions:

- Structured
- Textual
- Analog/Internet of Things (IoT)

Figure 1-1. Three types of data.

Structured data is comprised of transaction-generated data, such as from:

- Banking transactions
- ATM transactions
- Store purchases
- Airline and hotel reservations

Textual data contains the content of conversations and documents, such as from:

- Call center conversations
- Medical records
- Internet comments
- Contracts

Analog/IoT data consists of data generated by machines, such as from:

- Electric eyes
- Surveillance cameras
- Drones
- Temperature gauges

Although these three environments share a few common characteristics, they are very different in terms of volume, value, and access. It is as if the structured environment was the Antarctic, the textual environment was the Amazon River, and the analog/IoT environment was the Gobi Desert. Three very diverse environments.

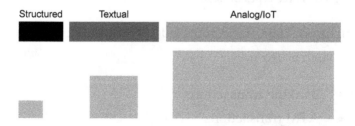

Figure 1-2. In terms of volume, the structured environment has the smallest amount of data, the textual environment has much more data than the structured environment, and the analog/IoT environment has the most data.

An interesting feature of the different environments is the percentage of data containing business value.

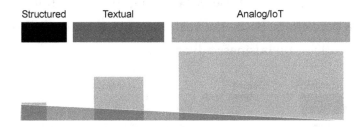

Structured   Textual   Analog/IoT

Figure 1-3. In terms of value, the structured environment has a very high percentage of data with potential business value. The textual environment contains quite a bit of business value. And the analog/IoT environment holds some business value.

Nearly all data in the structured environment can potentially have some business value. But there is a lot of data in the textual environment that does not have business value. A person sends an email talking about this week's football game. A guy calls a girl and asks her for a date. A person writes a blog on the Internet about how a hairdresser did their hair. Much data in the form of text has little or no business value.

Then there is analog/IoT data. Machines take many measurements in an automated manner. But only a few are important to the business. For example, consider a surveillance camera that overlooks a parking lot. Throughout the day, the surveillance camera takes a snapshot every 1/30 of a second. Most images show cars being parked, cars leaving the lot, or even an empty lot.

The image of a break-in to a car or an automobile accident occurs rarely. So analog/IoT data has the property of either being of no practical use or being highly useful. But based on a percentage basis, the vast majority of analog/IoT data is of little or no business advantage.

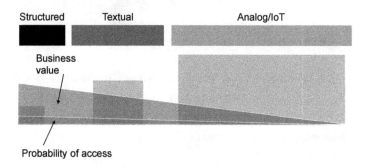

Figure 1-4. In terms of probability of access, there is a reasonable probability of access of data in the structured environment, a lesser probability of access of data in the textual environment, and an even lesser probability of access of data in the analog/IoT environment.

Managing data in the data lakehouse

When it comes to data management, storage mechanisms for these different types of data must be adjusted to the business value and probability of access. Data with high business value and a high probability of access needs to be stored on high-performance storage. Data with low business value and low probability of access needs to be stored in bulk storage.

Storing data in bulk storage does not mean that it cannot be accessed or analyzed if needed. However, the amount of work it takes to analyze data in bulk storage is considerably more than if the data were on high-performance storage. However, since the data is not used often, the price of having to struggle with bulk storage is paid infrequently. Stated differently, the cost of storage goes out of sight if there is an attempt to place all forms of storage in the data lakehouse on expensive, high-performance storage.

Evolution of the data lakehouse

So how did the data lakehouse evolve?

The evolution began with the realization that storing data from different media was useful for further analysis. And that, on occasion, it made sense to combine the data to enhance the analytical capabilities. At first, the idea was just to store the data.

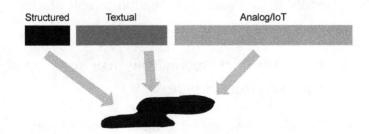

Figure 1-5. The data was stored in a structure called the data lake.

For a while, everything seemed to work just fine. Then, after many collections of data had been stored in the data lake, the organization realized that no one was using the data lake. Soon the data lake turned into a swamp. The swamp had no use. No one was using it and it was expensive to store the data.

What can be done to make the data found in the data lake useful? To start using the data in the data lake, you need to develop an analytical infrastructure over the data lake. This analytical infrastructure is the data lakehouse.

Analytical infrastructure

The analytical infrastructure consisted of many different types of information. One of the reasons for the diversity of information found in the analytical infrastructure was the wide diversity of data found in the data lake.

In addition to the diversity of data in the data lake, there is also diversity of analytical information in any processing environment.

Some of the kinds of information that make up the analytical infrastructure include:

- Metadata – description of fields, keys, indexes, tables, and databases

- Taxonomies – classifications of data
- Ontologies – groups of related taxonomies
- Data lineage – what transformations has the data undergone
- Source descriptions – where did the data originate
- Summarization descriptions – if the data was summarized, what algorithm was used
- Granularity definitions – what levels of detail are there
- Attribute definitions – what does an attribute mean
- Selection criteria – how data was included/excluded for selection
- Existing data models

The analytical infrastructure makes it easy for the analyst to find the data that is useful for analysis in the data lake.

Maintaining the data lakehouse

The data lakehouse is not built all at once. Instead, the data lakehouse evolves over time. Once the data lakehouse is built, it does not remain static. Instead, the data lakehouse is constantly revised. Data is always being added, amended, and archived.

Data lakehouse environment

One issue with data in the data lakehouse is whether we should place all data on a single platform. Although it is sometimes possible to keep the data lakehouse on a single platform, given the diversity of the data in the data lake it often makes sense to physically store the data separately. However, the data is still logically connected by the analytical infrastructure.

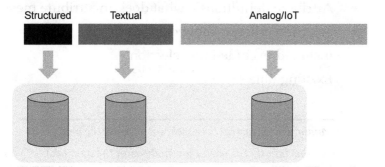

Figure 1-6. There is absolutely no reason why we need to house all the data in the data lakehouse on the same technology. Some data can be on the cloud, some on premise. The physical housing of the data is not a problem as long as the analytical infrastructure is built and maintained properly. Indeed there may be perfectly valid reasons why we house some data in one place and other data elsewhere.

When doing an analysis that combines more than one type of data, it may be necessary to extract the data that needs to be analyzed and to combine that data into a single physical pool of data.

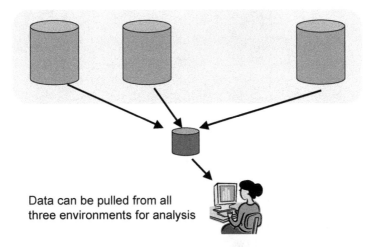

Data can be pulled from all
three environments for analysis

Figure 1-7. Extracting the data into a single smaller pool has many beneficial benefits.

Some of the benefits include:

- The data is focused
- The data is easier to work with
- The data can be isolated for heuristic processing

The data in the data lakehouse is data that is accessible,
believable, and usable for analytical processing.

CHAPTER 2

The Structured Environment

Efficiency of processing

The first architectural environment that evolved is the "structured environment." The structured environment starts with the occurrence of an event. The event may be the making of a sale. Or the initiation of a telephone call. Or the payment of a bill. Many different kinds of events trigger a need to keep track of the event. A business event occurs and the information about that event causes the creation of a computerized record. Typical information about a sale includes:

- The date of the sale
- The amount of the sale
- The item sold
- The location of the sale
- The form of payment
- The clerk handling the sale

We save the information about the event in a database record that exists within a database.

The term "structured" gets its name from the database records. Each of the records has the same basic structure. The only thing that differs from one record to the next is the content of the record itself. For example, one record is for your purchase. The next record is for the person in line behind you and their purchase. The next record is for the next purchase, and so forth. The only difference from one record to the next is the actual content of the record. By storing all the records in this fashion, the computer can process the records efficiently. The consistent structure of the records is built for the convenience of the speed of computer processing. When the computer reads and processes a record, the computer knows what data is placed where and how to process the data.

The data that is stored in the database is stored in the form of records. Each record has the same basic structure as the other records in the database. Of course, the record format varies from one database to the next. But the records in the same database all have the same structure.

Typically a record has a key and one or more attributes. Usually, the key uniquely identifies the record. A key might be Social Security Number, driver's license number, passport number, or employee number. The key usually has associated with it one or more attributes. When the data is normalized, the attribute depends on the key for its existence. Typical attributes for a person, for example, include:

- Name
- Age
- Gender
- Birth date
- Location of birth
- Marital status

The record typically has indexes that point directly to the data. The records are all placed inside a physical block of data. Without an index, the system must search for a record sequentially, having to look through all the data in the database. Indexes save a considerable amount of unnecessary processing.

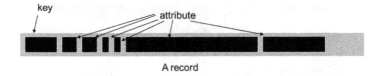

A record

Figure 2-1. The indexes allow the data to be accessed directly. Stated differently, when there is an index on a field, the index points directly to the database record. With an index, there is no need to search an entire database to find a record. A key is an index on a unique field, such as Social Security Number. An index can also be on a non-unique field, such as gender.

When building the database, the designer must consider that the index takes up space. And the index needs its own maintenance occasionally. Once the database record is built, it is placed into a physical block of data. The physical block of data can contain multiple records.

Another way that data can be organized without using an index is using a hasher or a randomizer. When a hasher is used, the system uses the value of the primary key of the record which is sent to the hasher. The hasher then uses the value of the key of the record to create an address. The address will be for the physical block of storage where the record is to be placed. The address that has been calculated is then used to place the record into the database.

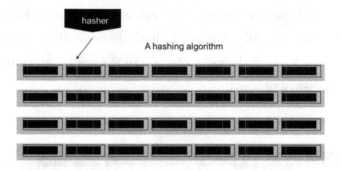

Figure 2-2. When it comes time for searching the database with a
    hasher, there is no system I/O (i.e., physical search of the data)
    required to find the database record. Instead, the address of the
    database record is located merely by looking at the value of the
    key and passing it through the hasher. The hasher then tells what
    physical block of data the record resides in. Doing these internal
    calculations through a hasher is much faster than physically
    searching the data.

As long as the hasher works efficiently, the hasher is faster than an index for searching for data. But the hasher can actually hurt performance during a "collision." A collision occurs when two or more records are identified by the hashing algorithm that are calculated to reside in the same address. Of course, two or more records cannot actually reside at the same address. Instead, one of the records must be placed in an overflow area. And finding the record in overflow becomes a slow and tedious process to retrieve.

The value of indexing and hashing is the ability to find and manipulate data in a database directly and efficiently. The ability to access data directly has some very profound implications for computer processing.

Advent of online systems

Before being able to process data directly, transactions and other computer processing had to be "batched." In batch processing, all activity is collected into a batch. Then, when enough transactions are collected, the transactions are executed. The need to batch all of the transactions meant that it took a lengthy amount of time to execute them. It may take anywhere from half an hour to 24 hours before running a transaction. The length of time required for running batch programs limited use of the computer for business-related activities. But with the advent of direct data access, whole new applications sprang to life. Online systems spawned the organization's ability to quickly service customer needs. Now there were reservation systems, ATM systems, airline processing, and more.

Online systems brought the ability to access data directly. And online systems further integrated the computer into the life of the business. With batch processing, the computer was an adjunct to the business. But with online systems, the computer became an integral part of the business. In some cases, the online system worked directly with the customer, and in other cases, the online system worked indirectly with the customer.

Once the online system started to impact the customer, online response time became a big issue. Online response time was an issue because when response time was not good, the customer became disgruntled, and the business suffered. A good example of online transaction processing is the ATM. When people use an ATM, they expect a very quick and very consistent response time. If the ATM experiences a slow transaction response time, the customer goes elsewhere and stops using the ATM.

Service level agreement

One of the ways that organizations assure themselves of good and consistent response time is to employ a "service level agreement" (SLA). An SLA is an agreement between the technician and the business person as to what constitutes expected performance. The SLA usually consists of a statement of performance goals during certain days and hours. The days covered by the SLA are the normal working days of the corporation, and the hours are the busiest during the business day. The SLA may (or may not) encompass off-hours, such as weekends and holidays.

SLA – service level agreement
Mon-Fri 8:00 am – 5:30 pm – 2 second
Mon- Fri – 6:00 pm – 7:30 am – 10 seconds
Weekend – 10 seconds (approximate)

Response time/
availability

Figure 2-3. In addition to system performance issues, the SLA usually covers the hours of availability for the online system, including when it is acceptable to have downtime and other outages.

Transactions

The method used to achieve a smooth and efficient flow of transactions through the online system is analogous to the smooth and regular flowing of sand through an hourglass.

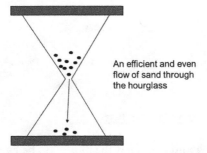

An efficient and even flow of sand through the hourglass

Figure 2-4. If you look at an hourglass filled with sand, you normally see that the sand has an efficient flow at the bottom of the hourglass, allowing it to measure time.

How is this consistent and efficient flow of sand through the hourglass achieved? The efficient flow of sand through the hourglass is achieved by having the grains of sand in the hourglass:

- Be small in size
- Be consistent in size

In other words, the flow of sand is efficient by filling the hourglass with uniformly small grains of sand.

The grains of sand are analogous to the transactions that run through the online system. The transactions run smoothly and efficiently when each transaction is small and the size of the transactions is consistent. The components of a transaction's performance include set up time, take down time, and line time. (Line time is the time it takes for the transaction to pass up and down the communications line.)

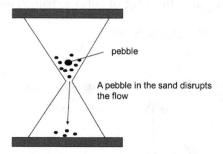

pebble

A pebble in the sand disrupts the flow

Figure 2-5. What would happen if the hourglass had a pebble mixed in with the grains of sand? The pebble would disrupt the smooth and efficient flow of sand through the hourglass. The closer the pebble got to the center of the hourglass, the more disruption.

However, the single largest factor relating to the performance of a transaction is queue time. Queue time is the amount of time it takes for a transaction to execute. As the online transaction goes into execution, it queues with the other transactions. The transaction executes after it passes through the queue.

The best way to minimize transaction queue time is to ensure that each transaction is small and uniform. So what constitutes a large transaction from a small transaction? The amount of time it takes to execute a transaction is the main factor in determining its size.

We need to understand the dynamics inside the computer to understand how long it takes for a transaction to execute. There are two relevant speeds: electronic speeds and mechanical speeds. Electronic speeds are about 1,000 faster than mechanical speeds.

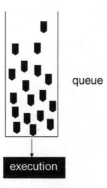

Figure 2-6. If there are many transactions in the queue, the transaction has to wait on all of those transactions in front of it to execute before it can execute.

To illustrate the speed difference, suppose you made a trip from Dallas to Chicago. You fly from Dallas to Oklahoma City. You then ride your bicycle to Tulsa. Then you catch a plane from Tulsa to Des Moines. Then bike from Des Moines to Sioux City. Then catch a plane from Sioux City to Chicago.

Does it help on this trip to catch a faster jet plane? The jet plane's speed is almost irrelevant to the optimization of the speed of the trip. Improving the speed of the airplane helps a little but not much. What would really help is to avoid all the bike trips, or at least go by car rather than bike. Reducing the number of bike trips or speeding them up helps the efficiency of the trip.

Every time the programmer calls for the program to get data from disk storage, the programmer has slowed down execution from electronic to mechanical speeds. Such an activity is called an "I/O" or input/output operation.

Of course, the programmer can have the database placed inside main memory. Placing all of the data inside main memory reduces I/O. But there is only so much room inside main memory. Main memory is also much more expensive than disk storage.

Another factor affecting performance is the need for transaction integrity during transaction processing. For example, transaction A enters the computer and searches for a customer's bank balance. Transaction A finds the record and is busy transacting the business of determining if a customer can cash a check. The balance shows $500 when transaction A asks the system. However, immediately after transaction A has accessed the account balance, transaction B subtracts $400 from the account. The system tells the bank teller that the transaction can continue when the bank balance is only $100.

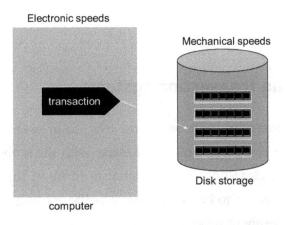

Figure 2-7. The fewer times the programmer needs to stop and go to disk storage, the faster the program will run. The number of I/Os determines the program's size.

More than one transaction can work on the same data simultaneously is a problem that the integrity of processing solves. To prevent this kind of misinformation, transaction A must lock the records being processed while transaction A controls the record. Then when transaction A completes, transaction B can do whatever business it needs to do. Transaction B will lock the data while it is operating on the data.

The mechanism needed to ensure transaction integrity is called "record locking." Record locking is an essential component of online transaction processing.

In the face of many transactions attempting to execute simultaneously, transaction integrity can become a problem for performance. This is especially true when a transaction locks many records as part of its processing.

Creating transaction systems

Transactions are built based on the requirements of the end-user. The designer/analyst starts with the scope of the project. A clear definition of what is to be in the system and what is not to be in the system is the starting point for the development process.

Next, the designer/analyst interviews the end-user to determine the business requirements. The data going into the system, the processing of that data, and the data coming out of the system are identified. After the requirements are synthesized and organized, the designer/analyst starts system design. This development cycle is called the waterfall approach or Software Development Lifecycle (SDLC). Most transactions were built using this waterfall design approach.

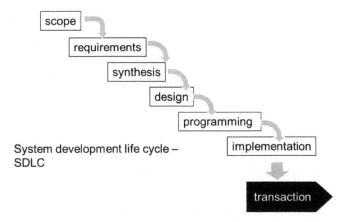

Figure 2-8. For many organizations, the waterfall approach to development brought about great success.

Soon the organization was building many systems. New systems started to spring up like weeds in the springtime.

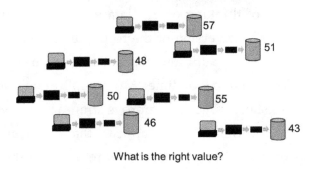

What is the right value?

Figure 2-9. Then one day, the organization realized that the same data existed in many places. The problem was that the same element of data had different values in different systems. The organization did not have a problem finding data. The organization had a hard finding the *right* data.

Furthermore, trying to go back and reconcile the many different renditions of data across many different systems was challenging. Even after a long, complex, laborious effort, the designer/analyst was still not sure of the correct value of data. The organization learned the lesson of the need for data integrity across the enterprise.

Enter the data warehouse

The need for integrity and believability of data over the spectrum of many application systems led to the architectural construct called the data warehouse. The data warehouse could identify and make publicly available the correct value of data throughout the corporation.

Another way of thinking of the data warehouse is that it became the "single version of the truth" for data found in the corporation. In addition, the data warehouse stored data for long periods of time. Most applications stored data for a short time to improve transaction system performance. At first glance, it appears that data is merely copied over from the application environment to the data warehouse. Indeed, some data is copied over. But a transformation process takes place where data is decidedly not copied to the data warehouse.

The transformation process is necessary and important. Through the transformation process, application data becomes corporate data.

As an example of the transformations made in moving data from applications to corporate data, suppose there are four applications. Each application designer has chosen their unique means of representing data in their application. Each application has a different way of representing data: m/f, male/female, x/y, and 1/0. The transformations shown in this example are the tip of the iceberg when transforming data. In truth, nearly all transformations are very complex and challenging.

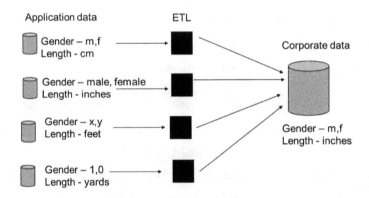

Figure 2-10. To be placed in the data warehouse, there must be a corporate method of representing gender. The data warehouse designer chooses to represent gender as m/f. Where gender appears as m/f, the data is copied from the application to the warehouse. But in the other applications, the different representations of gender are converted to m/f. In making this transformation, application data becomes corporate data.

Transformations are made with the help of a corporate data model. The data warehouse solved the problems of:

- Identifying how data integrity ought to be addressed
- Creating a place where data could be stored for a lengthy amount of time
- Building a foundation for building the corporate understanding of data

ETL (Extract, Transform, and Load) is an essential component of the data warehouse environment. ETL is the software that does the transformation of data. Not only did ETL expedite the building of the data warehouse, ETL also expedited the process of maintaining the programs that accomplished the transformations.

However, the data warehouse introduces a new set of problems. One of those problems was what to do about the large volumes of data within the warehouse. Another problem was the need to customize data for different organizations. The typical areas needing their own customized data warehouse version were marketing, sales, finance, and management. In addition, on occasion, human resources needed its own customized data and engineering needed its own customized data.

The data mart was built using the architectural structure of dimensional modeling. Dimensional modeling used such things as the star join, different dimensions, and fact tables.

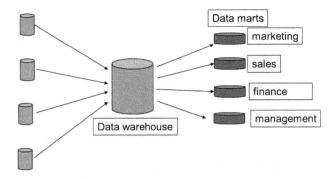

Figure 2-11. In response to the need for a customized data warehouse, another architectural structure appeared: the data mart. Data could be taken from the data warehouse and placed into the data mart. The data mart could then be shaped to specific project needs. And as long as the source of all data for the data mart was the data warehouse, reconciliation was easy to do.

Storing data over time

One of the features of data warehousing is that the data warehouse is useful for storing historical data. Before data warehousing, there really was no convenient place to store historical data. One of the by-products of this phenomenon of storing data over time was that data warehouses started to grow to very large sizes. It was typical for a data warehouse to hold five and even ten years of data.

As data warehouses started to grow in size, the data warehouse manager started to notice a phenomenon. That phenomenon was that only a small part of the data warehouse was used for analytical purposes with any consistency. Most of the data just sat there in the data warehouse, untouched. The data that was never used was called dormant data.

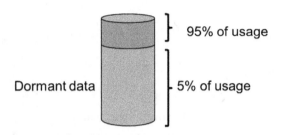

Figure 2-12. The data warehouse analyst discovered the phenomenon known as dormant data.

For many reasons, the dormant data in a data warehouse became a burden. The cost of the dormant storage was significant and the added dormant data slowed down certain analytical processes.

So a different solution was needed.

The evolution from a standard data warehouse to an actively used data warehouse involved:

- identifying what data was active and what data was dormant
- moving the dormant data to a form of bulk storage
- Periodically archiving data from the active portion of the data warehouse to the inactive portion

The end result was still a data warehouse. But the data warehouse was now spread over multiple technologies.

CHAPTER 3

The Textual Environment

There is a vast amount of data within the organization in the form of text. Based on our experience, 85%-90% of the data within an organization is in the form of text, such as emails, Web pages, memos, and contracts. Computer systems can certainly store text. But as long as text is stored in the form of text, its benefits cannot be realized. Relational Database Management Systems (RDBMS) handle highly-structured data, and text is not structured. Text is not normally placed into a RDBMS because:

- Text is very complex. The same word can mean lots of things
- There are many languages, such as English, Spanish, and Mandarin
- There is slang
- People often misspell words

There are lots of barriers to being able to read text and produce a database from the text. The largest barrier is context.

Context

To understand the meaning of text, you must also understand context. And context is a difficult subject because context is understood external to the text itself. As an example of what it means to understand context outside of the text, consider two men are talking about a lady, and one says to the other, "She's hot."

Now, what is meant by "she's hot." One possibility is that he finds the lady attractive. Another possibility is that it is Houston, Texas in July, and the lady is sweating and physically hot. A third possibility is that the men are doctors. One doctor has just taken her temperature, and she has a temperature of 104 degrees Fahrenheit. In addition, she has a fever and is internally hot. To make sense of the words "she's hot," you need to know:

- Are the men doctors?
- Is the conversation occurring in Houston, Texas in July?
- Do they find the lady attractive?

Those factors are external to the text, "She's hot." To understand the context, you must know many things that are not directly related to the spoken or written text.

The understanding of the external context of the words allows the words to be understood.

Textual disambiguation

So what's the problem with just storing a lot of information in the form of text? The problem is that the text must be manually read to process that text. And reading anything manually is a tedious, mistake-ridden, slow, expensive exercise. If you want to digest a large amount of text, you need to do it in an automated manner.

An automated process for reading documents, organizing the information in documents, and placing documents in the form of a database allows the documents to be read and processed without considering the number of documents. So how is it possible to read and process all of these documents? To make sense of what has been read, the computer needs to read the documents and know how to read and interpret the words being read.

We need to disambiguate the text when loading the text into a database. Disambiguation of text implies that the automation mechanism understands and manages both the text and its context. Only after the text has been disambiguated can the automation proceed.

So how is text read and disambiguated? The answer is that there are a variety of techniques. Because of the variability and complexity of text, more than one method for handling text is required.

In many ways, textual disambiguation is like an orchestra playing a beautiful song. One moment the violins play. Then the flutes play. Then the cellos. Then the drums. The result is beautiful music when all of the instruments are led by a skillful conductor. If the flutes were paying Yankee Doodle Dandy, the violins were playing a concerto, the cellos were playing Yesterday, and the piano was playing the Star-Spangled Banner, the result would be a disruptive and incongruous noise. It is only when the instruments play together with the help of a conductor that beautiful music results.

Managing the disambiguation of text is much the same as conducting an orchestra. The are many approaches that must be combined to make sense of the text that is being read and processed.

Proximity analysis

A simple way that text can be plucked of a raw format and placed into a database is by looking at the text in proximity to other text. For example, if a person says the "Dallas cowboys" it is likely that a person thinks of a professional football team in Texas. But if a person says "Dallas" on page one and then three pages later says "cowboys" it is likely that the person thinks of something else entirely different. The proximity of words together then makes a big difference in interpreting the meaning of the words.

Textual syntactic patterns

Another way text and its context are determined is by discovering the text's patterns. For example, if a person writes digits in the form 999-99-9999, the person is likely referring to a Social Security Number. But if a person refers to the string of digits 999-999-9999, the digits likely refer to a US telephone number. In some cases, the text's pattern is a clue as to its meaning and context.

Homographic resolution

Yet another way text and its meaning are derived is through homographic resolution. Homographic resolution is the process of determining the meaning of a word or phrase by finding out who wrote the word.

For example, consider the reading and disambiguation of doctor's notes. In the doctor's notes, the term "ha" is encountered. If the person who wrote the notes was a cardiologist, the term "ha" likely refers to heart attack. But if the person who wrote the notes was an endocrinologist, "ha" would refer to hepatitis A. Or if the doctor who wrote the notes was a general practitioner, the term "ha" would refer to headache.

With homographic resolution, there is a need to know who wrote the text to be able to decipher its meaning and context. To process the doctor's notes properly, it is important to do homographic resolution. Because if you don't make the proper interpretation, you may mistake "ha" for headache when the intent is heart attack. And making such a mistake could be disastrous.

Inline contextualization

But some text is predictable. (Indeed, most text is spontaneous and very unpredictable.) For example, contracts have a large preponderance of predictable text because lawyers heavily use the practice of creating boilerplate. In a boilerplate, text is written out once and then reused in many places. The lawyer creates a standard contract. Then when a sale is made, the salesperson merely places the person's name in the proper place in the boilerplate contract.

In using boilerplate, text becomes quite predictable. The same text in the same order appears in contract after contract. Once text becomes predictable, it is possible to use the technique of inline contextualization.

With inline contextualization, we find a beginning delimiter and an ending delimiter. Then those delimiters are used to "trap" text between them.

For example, a contract says "...we agree to purchase the product. Purchaser name ...... on this day of...." The words "purchaser name" would be the beginning delimiter and the words "on this day" would be the ending delimiter. Whatever name appears between the delimiters is understood to be the name of the customer. It is noteworthy that predictable text occurs in many other places than contracts. For example, predictable text occurs in laboratory reports and in other legal documents.

Taxonomical resolution

Yet another way that we recognize words in raw text along with their context is by using taxonomical resolution. In taxonomical resolution, a taxonomy of words are created. Typical taxonomies might be for trees, bushes, and flowers. The taxonomy for a tree might include an elm, oak, pecan, or mesquite. The taxonomy for a bush might include an azalea or rose. The taxonomy for a flower might include a tulip, marigold, or iris. The raw text is read and when a word appears that is in one of the taxonomies, the word and its context are recognized.

In truth, there are many other ways to identify text and the context of text. Disambiguation of text takes many forms. Textual ETL's job is to recognize when an approach is needed. Like the conductor directing the symphony orchestra, textual ETL directs different algorithms needed to disambiguate text. These techniques that have been described are but a few of the many techniques that constitute textual disambiguation.

Database structure

The database created from processing and disambiguating the text can take many forms. But the basic form of the database that is created looks like:

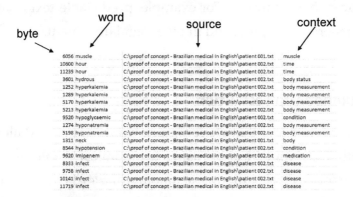

Figure 3-1. There are the fields of data that indicate the byte address of the word, the word that has been encountered, the source document of the word, and the context of the word.

Even though the database looks like a simple relational database, the analyst has opened up the possibility of processing an unlimited amount of data by placing the text in this database. Stated differently, as long as the data remains in its textual format, it can only be processed manually. But once the text is placed in a database format, it can be processed infinitely.

Creating the database is just the first step in the analytical process. The basic database sets the stage for other kinds of analysis, including:

- Sentiment analysis
- Correlative analysis
- Other forms of analysis

Identifying information

When we transform text into a database, there is useful identifying information associated with the text. For example, when you read the Internet and encounter Yelp, you find that the free-form comments found in Yelp are preceded by identifying information. Identifying information is often quite useful in connecting the text to structured data.

For a variety of reasons, many organizations need to have their text identified before any processing can occur. Certain fields of text are obvious, such as name, Social Security Number and telephone number. But there are other fields that can lead to identification. These secondary fields include gender, race, age, and other similar data.

Date: Jan 3, 2022
Product: generator
Rating: 2
Location: Cincinnati, Ohio

"the contract 134-9087 clearly states that the date for delivery is July 20, 2020. The generator – AS12-9082 – was not delivered to the address on the invoice. This means that the contract is null and void."

Figure 3-2. Not all text has this identifying information. But when identifying information exists, it is quite useful to be able to include it as an attachment to the freeform text.

Negation

One of the features of processing text before placing it in a database is the necessity of being able to recognize negation. For example, when the doctor says, "the patient does not have tuberculosis," it is important to notice that this is a negation. If the mechanism doing the disambiguation did not recognize negation, the inference might well be that the patient had tuberculosis. And that, of course, would have been the entirely incorrect conclusion.

> "the contract 134-9087 clearly states that the date for delivery is July 20, 2020. The generator – AS12-9082 – was ▓ : ▓▓▓▓ to the address on the invoice. This means that the contract is null and void."

Figure 3-3. It is not enough just to be able to read and interpret text. You must be able to read and interpret negation as well.

Acronyms

Another important feature of reading and interpreting text is the feature of being able to read and interpret acronyms. Some professions, such as the medical profession, make liberal use of acronyms.

In the case of medical records, acronyms are further confusing because different specialties of medicine use the same acronym for different meanings.

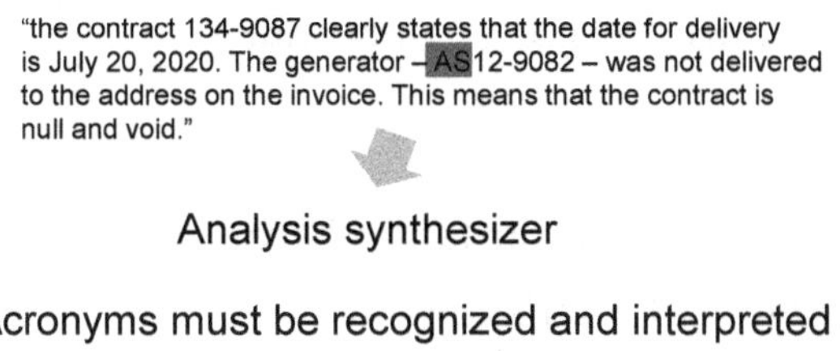

"the contract 134-9087 clearly states that the date for delivery is July 20, 2020. The generator – AS 12-9082 – was not delivered to the address on the invoice. This means that the contract is null and void."

Analysis synthesizer

Acronyms must be recognized and interpreted

Figure 3-4. Being able to disambiguate acronyms is absolutely essential to the entire process of textual disambiguation.

Benefits from understanding text

So who needs to be able to read text and analyze text with standard analytical software? The answer is practically everyone. Some of the places where text exists and could benefit from being placed into a database include:

- Medical records
- Hearing the voice of the customer
- Understanding corporate contracts
- Reading and understanding warranties
- Reading and understanding insurance claims

Text pervades the corporations and there is tremendously useful information wrapped up in the form of text. Text needs to become part of the decision-making process. Text can be visualized when it is placed into the form of a database. Visualization can take many forms, including knowledge graphs, Pareto charts, and pie charts. There are many ways to visualize data once in the form of a database.

Visualization is important because it is through visualization that management starts understanding the data.

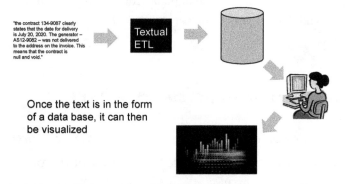

Once the text is in the form of a data base, it can then be visualized

Figure 3-5. Management simply cannot understand results in the form of a database. But once the database is visualized, then management starts to see the value of the data. And text cannot be visualized unless it is put into the form of a database.

Another important value of placing text into a database is that once the text has been transformed and placed into a database, it can then be combined and compared with other data in a database. By combining data from different sources, the analyst can start to do analytics in a manner that he/she has never been able to do before.

CHAPTER 4

Analog/IoT Data Architecture

D ata comes from everywhere. Data comes from transactions. Data comes from observations. Data comes from records created as an event unfolds. One of the most pervasive and potentially useful places that data comes from is machines. Machines generate a significant and important volume of data.

Examples

Drones collect data, telephones collect data, watches collect data, automobiles collect data, and so forth. The sources of machine-generated data are many. To understand how a machine generates data, let's consider some examples.

A steel manufacturer

Machines generate a lot of data in a manufacturing plant. For a steel manufacturer, raw materials are placed into a pot or kettle. The raw materials are heated to a very hot temperature. The unwanted material is poured off.

Figure 4-1. The remaining material is poured into a set of molds that can withstand heat.

The molds then move the steel across a long conveyer belt. At this point, the steel starts to cool and its shape is formed. The output from the mill is then rolled into sheets. As the sheets of steel are formed, the steel passes by an electric eye. The electric eye measures a lot of things about the steel, including:

- temperature
- width of the sheet of steel
- chemical composition

The measurements are made every 12 inches as the steel passes on the conveyer belt. Much information is collected for a given steel heat (a batch of steel).

If a problem arises, an engineer can use the measurements to determine the nature of the problem and how it can be fixed.

A surveillance camera

Consider a surveillance camera for a parking lot. The surveillance camera takes snapshots of the lot throughout the day and the night. Typically, the camera takes a snapshot every 1/30th of a second.

Figure 4-2. The camera records the comings and goings of the cars in the parking lot. Even when the lot is empty, the surveillance camera takes pictures of the lot.

Most of the time, the pictures taken by the camera are uneventful, such as pictures of an empty parking lot or cars routinely being parked or driven away. However, in the eventuality of an accident or robbery, surveillance camera pictures become very valuable. As a percentage of the number of pictures taken, less than .01% are probably useful. However, the pictures that are useful are *really* interesting and *really* useful.

A railroad electric eye

A rancher has an agreement with the railroad company that every time a railroad car passes through the rancher's land, the railroad will pay the rancher a predetermined amount. The railroad places an electric eye on the land, and the electric eye counts the cars that pass over the land. At the end of the month, the number of cars are tallied and a check is sent to the rancher.

Figure 4-3. Throughout the day, the electric eye does nothing. Only when a train passes by is the electric eye activated and the cars counted.

Data characteristics

Some event occurs and the event triggers the collection of records of data. In the case of a steel manufacturer, a batch of steel is manufactured. Then as the steel is cooled, it is measured. In the case of a surveillance camera, the recording is reset every 24 hours. In the case of an electric eye counting railroad cars, the event is triggered by the passing by of a train crossing the land.

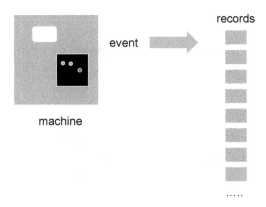

Figure 4-4. An event occurs and the machine starts to record information.

Machine-generated data has several important characteristics.

Volume

Machine-generated data leads to many records. Relative to structured data and textual data, two to three orders of magnitude of data can be produced by machines as measured against data produced by transactions or text.

The large data volumes benefit the data scientist because they can do detailed low-level analytics and examine many different variables. However, working with large volumes of machine-generated data is like trying to move a skyscraper rather than moving a rock. Indeed, the volume of data produced by a machine becomes one of the limiting factors in managing machine-produced data.

Probability of access

To manage machine-generated data successfully, it is useful to divide the data into two classes:

- Regularly occurring data that has a known use
- Irregularly occurring data where the uses of the data are unknown or unexplored

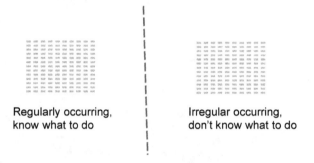

Regularly occurring, know what to do

Irregular occurring, don't know what to do

One way to divide analog/IoT data

Figure 4-5. Another way of stating these two classes is data with a high probability of access and data with a low probability of access.

The division of data according to the probability of access is sometimes called the segmentation of data. The segmentation of data has several very beneficial effects:

- Data can be integrated and compared with other data
- Data can be stored on different storage technologies. Data that has a low probability of access can be stored on slower, less expensive

storage. The fact that it is stored on less expensive technology does not mean it cannot be accessed and analyzed. It just means that when access and analysis are done, the analysis is done more slowly. And data with a high probability of access can be stored on more expensive storage. And the more expensive technology can be accessed quickly and with agility.

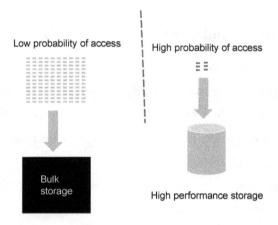

Figure 4-6. As a rule, there is usually a lot of data that has a low probability of access. And there is usually a lot less data that has a high probability of access.

How does the analyst determine the probability of access of data? Perhaps the best source of determining the probability of access is finding an experienced engineer who regularly looks at and analyzes the data. The experienced engineer will immediately know what fields of data and type of data is important, and which data is not important.

Another likely source for determining the probability of access of data is an experienced end-user analyst who is familiar with the data and what can be done with it. A final method for determining the probability of access of machine-generated data is by trial and error. Trial and error always works. But it is expensive and time-consuming to execute. It should always be a last resource.

Internal/external data

Another useful way to divide the data is through the differences between internally and externally generated data. Internally-generated data is data that the organization generates. Externally-generated data is data that is generated outside the organization. Externally-generated data can come from anywhere. Some of the common sources include:

- Weather data
- Economic data from the WSJ
- Demographic data from the bureau of statistics
- Inflation data from the department of commerce

Analyzing data

Once we store the data, we can then analyze the data. Experience has shown that one of the traits that leads to success is knowing the need for the data before starting analysis. Of course, it is possible to simply take some data and start the analysis just to see what is in there. But often, no value comes from analyzing data for the sake of analyzing data.

Know what business value is being sought before the analysis begins.

Patterns

The analyst is looking for patterns within the data. The discovery of patterns can lead to the practice of improving business practices. The discovery of coincidental patterns coming from different data sources is even more interesting.

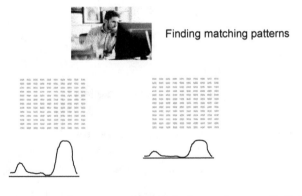

Finding matching patterns

Figure 4-7. We can draw powerful conclusions when we find the same pattern in different data sources.

Note that the different sources of data can be widely dispersed. One source can be internally-generated data. Another source can be externally-generated data. It is almost always a mistake to blindly search machine-generated data for patterns of other interesting data. If you don't know what you are looking for, blindly doing analysis rarely yields positive results.

Correlation or cause and effect

When we discover matching patterns of data, we can conclude:

- The data can be merely correlated, or
- The data can signal a cause and effect relationship

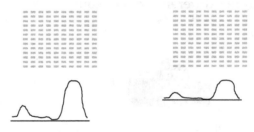

Corelative or cause and effect?

Figure 4-8. There are true cause-and-effect relationships.

As a simple example of mere correlation of data, for years there was a relationship between the football league that won the Super Bowl and the rise or fall of the stock market. When one league won, the stock market would rise. When the other league won, the stock market would fall. While these values correlated, there was no underlying reason for the correlation. It was merely a coincidental correlation. For example, the manipulation of the supply of money across the nation has a very close relationship to the inflation rate. When the government decides to produce money, it is predictable that the inflation rate will rise. Stated differently, the government can create inflation by manipulating the money supply.

Heuristic analysis

In most cases, we analyze machine-generated data with heuristics.

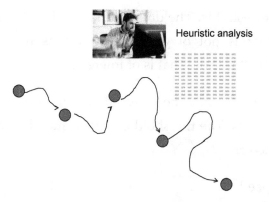

Figure 4-9. The analysis begins by looking for some kind of answer. Once the first analysis completes, the second starts based on the learnings from the first analysis. This learning process with each analysis iteration continues until we reach the final answer. In some cases, of course, no final answer is reached.

One feature of heuristic analysis is that the analyst does not know when the analysis will end at the outset. And the analyst does not know if there will even be an answer to the questions in consideration.

Making sense of machine-generated data

There are many techniques for managing machine-generated data. The first and most basic is the separation of data by the probability of access and usage of the data.

Another technique in managing machine-generated data is to look at the data according to thresholds. There can be a minimum threshold, a minimum and maximum threshold, or other thresholds. The data that lies inside the threshold is data that is not of great interest. It is the data that exceeds the threshold that is of interest.

The threshold can be created along one or more measurements. The threshold can be formed by examining factors such as:

- Speed
- Heat
- Length of time
- Sequence
- Weight
- Conformance to standards

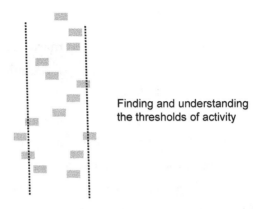

Finding and understanding
the thresholds of activity

**Figure 4-10. The exact parameters used to form the threshold are
strictly up to the analyst and the data being examined.**

Another important consideration in the management of machine data is the consideration of combining machine-generated data with other machine-generated data. While combining different bodies of data can certainly be done, we must consider the volumes of data. Another consideration when managing machine-generated data is how the data is logically connected. For there to even be a merging of the data, there needs to be some data that can be used as a connector.

However, there may or may not be a connector at all. For example, connecting weather data and sales data has little obvious connection. In this case, it may not be able to connect the data through a means other than one of the universal connectors, such as time or geography.

Other data may have a very loose connection. One of the very unreliable connectors of data is the connection made based on a person's name. The problem, however, is that a person's name is not unique. There are many John Smiths and Mary Adams in the world. Or John Smith's name appears as John Smith in one place and as J T Smith elsewhere. Nevertheless, sometimes a person's name may be the only way to connect data. But a person's name is a weak connector of data. Yet, we can connect other data based on a very strong connection. For example, data may contain fields such as Social Security Number, passport number, employee number, driver's license number, and so forth.

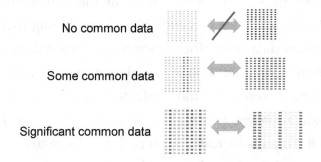

Figure 4-11. When the analyst decides to connect data coming from different sources, one consideration is the data that is common to both types of data that we use to combine the data.

Data capture

An important consideration in creating machine-generated data is how the data even finds its way into the databases of the corporation. Some of the considerations include:

- What data to select and what data to exclude?
- What fields to select and what fields to reject?
- Has the data been edited at the point of capture?
- What data quality criteria have been exercised?
- When has the data been captured?
- Has the source of the data been identified?
- Has the event causing the capture of data been fully documented and described?

Data archival

One of the most important considerations of managing machine-generated data is that of archiving the data. Machine-generated data is like every other form of data in that it loses its value over time.

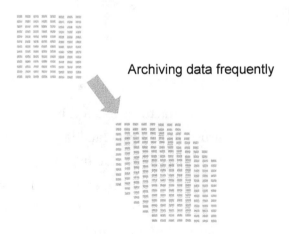

Archiving data frequently

Figure 4-12. It is wasteful and unprofessional to store machine-generated data past its point of usefulness.

Value of data samples

The insistence of looking at the entire set of data for every analysis instead of a sample set increases:

- Costs
- Time to do analysis
- Amount of data to process

Indeed, using data samples can greatly expedite analysis and reduce the analysis cost. Of course, one of the things the analyst must be wary of is the bias that is interjected into data when choosing the sample set. In some cases, the bias becomes a real issue. In other cases, the bias of the sample is simply not an issue.

Examples

An airbag manufacturer

Consider an airbag manufacturer located in Arizona as an example of making use of analysis facilitated by machine-generated data. The airbag manufacturer has to produce explosives as part of the manufacturing process. The explosives are what activate the airbag in the case of an accident. So, a regular part of the manufacture of airbags is the manufacture of explosives.

The manufacturer noticed that, on occasion, the explosives became unstable. When the explosives became unstable, they were dangerous to handle. Indeed, serious accidents were caused by the instability of the explosives.

So the manufacturer decided to find out what was causing the instability of the explosive. The air bag manufacturer looked at such things as:

- The quality of the chemicals used in making the explosive
- The storage of the explosive
- The way the explosive was being made
- The mixture process of the explosive

Nothing the manufacturer looked at seemed to relate to the explosives' instability. Then one day, almost accidentally, the manufacturer decided to look at the weather. For the most part, the weather in Arizona is dry and warm. But occasionally, a front appears from off of the Mexican coast. When this happens, there is a rise in the humidity of the air. The coincidence of the periods of time when the explosives were unstable correlated exactly to the periods of humidity in the air. This correlation was done by comparing the dates of the patterns of instability of the explosive with the periods of humidity in Arizona.

Once that correlation was found, the analyst knew the cause of the instability.

A steel manufacturer

Recall the steel manufacturer we discussed earlier in this chapter. The steel was measured in 12-inch intervals as it came off the mill. The measurements were placed in two locations based on the probability of access. Data that was frequently correlated to high quality was placed in one location. Data that was not associated with the quality of the steel production was placed in another location.

If there were ever circumstances where it was necessary to look at the low probability of data access, such a search could be conducted. But in general, only the high probability of data access was ever used.

When an analysis was done, the engineer looked for such things as:

- The heat of the mixture
- The removal of impurities
- The pouring rate
- The cooling rate

By examining the known factors in steel production, the analyst used analysis to improve the quality of the manufacturer's final product.

CHAPTER 5

The Data Lakehouse Canonical Model

There are lots of data and types of data in the data lakehouse. Trying to understand and keep track of the data is a full-time job.

Canonical data model

One of the ways that the data from the lakehouse can be organized and understood is by creating a canonical data model.

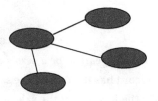

Figure 5-1. The canonical data model has many uses, including synthesizing data, organizing data into different types of relationships, and comparing one type of data to another. But perhaps the most valuable use of a canonical data model is that the model allows the designer/analyst to see across large vistas of data.

Connectors

However, the big challenge in creating the canonical data model is that the data in the data lakehouse is fundamentally very different. The data lakehouse holds three types of data: structured, textual, and analog/IoT. These different types of data are:

- Collected differently
- Stored differently
- Organized differently

This great diversity of types of data makes creating a canonical model challenging to create and maintain over time.

Structured	Text	Analog/IoT
Sale	"I was walking my dog	Snapshot date
Sale	and a yellow Porsche	Time
Sale	drove by. I recognized	1:02
Sale	the driver – it was the	1:06
Sale	actor James Wood..."	1:12
Sale		1:17
		1:23
......		....

Figure 5-2. Structured data appears to be a series of sales that a retailer makes. Each sale record has the date of the sale, the item sold, the amount of the sale, the location of the sale, and so forth, captured in a record. A sale record occurs, and the records created are placed in a structured environment. The textual environment is made from instances of text. The text may be from a phone call, the Internet, an email, a contract, and so forth. A machine creates analog/IoT data. The machine may be a surveillance camera, an electric eye, a temperature gauge, a clock, or any other device.

Despite these fundamental differences in how data is collected and organized, creating a canonical data model for the data lakehouse may still be worthwhile.

To create a canonical data model, it is necessary to have some common data among the different environments. For example, suppose you have a missile shot generating telemetry data and in another database you have the receipts for the meals served at a restaurant. There is no common data between these two events/environments, so creating a canonical data model would be difficult. In fact, it is even questionable why you would want to try to connect these two environments.

Now consider another set of environments. A chip manufacturer makes semiconductor chips in a computer that a vendor sells to a customer. Now there is a common thread between the different environments. In this case, it is possible to create a canonical data model for the data in the data lakehouse based on the commonality of data found in the computer.

To create a canonical model across the data lakehouse, you need to have one or more elements of data that are common to all the different types of data

Figure 5-3. There is a single thread of data that connects the three different environments.

Having single (or multiple) connectors among the different environments is the best way to connect the different environments. But in many cases, there are no such connectors. When there is no common connector of data, we can use a universal common connector. The most basic common connectors of data include:

- Time
- Geography
- Dollar amount

Every event has a moment in time to which it is related. And every activity that has occurred has a location. For example, suppose you wanted to connect the output of a steel manufacturer with the doctor's notes with the sales of ice cream bars. These three very unrelated activities have no internal data connection. But all three diverse activities have an occurrence time and place. So regardless of anything else, these unrelated activities can be related using time or geography.

Dollar amount is a little more problematic because not all events and activities have a dollar amount. There are, however, other universal common connectors. When it comes to human beings, for example, an analysis can be done using:

- Race
- Age
- Gender

- Smoking
- Alcohol consumption
- Weight
- Medications taken

So it is always possible to connect data based on a universal connector. The problem is that the connection made does not make much sense in many cases. If there is a much more concrete connector of data, that works better than a universal common connector.

Much more useful is a common generic connector. For example, a manufacturer makes a box of cereal. A merchant sells the box of cereal. And the consumer eats the cereal and wants to tell everyone how delicious it is. In this case, there is a generic common connector of a type of cereal. The level of detail does not go any further than that. There is no specific box of cereal. The cereal is generic.

Nevertheless, the box of cereal generically connects the different environments.

There is a way to connect the different environments. Once that means of connection is done, the different environments can be related to each other.

Yet another example of connecting data directly is through a very specific, non-generic type of data. Suppose a chip maker produces chips. Each chip has unique information stored on it. For example, the chip has the manufacturer information, manufacture lot, machine used in the manufacturing process, and a unique chip number. The chip is then installed in a computer, along with many other chips. The vendor that sells the computer one day discovers that the computer adds 1 + 1 and gets 3. This is a fundamental error caused by a defective chip. The vendor takes the computer apart and finds the defective chip.

In this case, it is possible to tie the world of the manufacturer and the vendor together. There is a detailed, specific linkage between the two environments.

Now consider another example. There is a restaurant chain that has a lot of customers. The restaurant chain would like to know what customers say about their restaurant. The restaurant wants to improve user satisfaction with food and service. On the Internet is information about the location of the restaurant. And there is a date that the comment was submitted. The information on the Internet then allows the consumer to say anything they want. The consumer may have loved the food, hated the food, not liked the server, and so forth. By reading the comments and relating the comments back to a specific location, the analyst can connect the consumer to the specific restaurant.

Note, however, that there is a limited scope of connectivity in this case as there is no way to know the manufacturer.

Therefore, the scope of analysis will not include the farmer or rancher that provided the food.

Individual canonical data models

Another approach to creating and managing the canonical model is the ability to create individual canonical data models for each of the different environments.

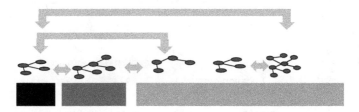

Figure 5-4. Once we create the individual canonical models for each environment, we next compare and contrast the different models.

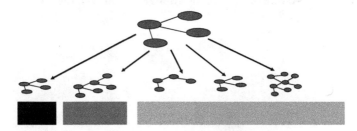

Figure 5-5. By comparing and contrasting the different data models, the larger canonical data model for the organization starts to take shape.

The more specific the data connectors and the more environments the connecting data is found in, the better.

Different strengths of connectivity

The following figure shows that there are different strengths of connectivity that are at the basis of the canonical data model.

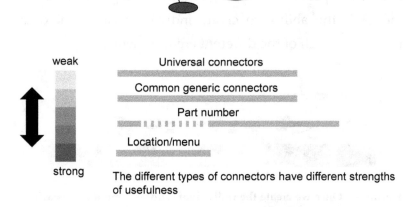

The different types of connectors have different strengths of usefulness

Figure 5-6. As a rule of thumb, the stronger the model, the more useful it is.

CHAPTER 6

Data Warehouse and Data Lakehouse

The origins of the data warehouse date back to the day when there were multiple applications, each containing their own version of the same data element. The problem was that the same data element did not have the same value. Trying to figure out what data was the correct data was a challenging task.

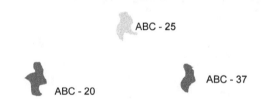

Figure 6-1. A world of chaos.

Enter the data warehouse

From this confusion of data came the data warehouse. The data warehouse facilitated the transformation from application data to corporate data. One feature of the data warehouse was the process of Extract, Transform, and

Load (ETL). ETL transforms data from application to corporate data.

Another feature of the data warehouse was that the data warehouse contained a long history of data—five to ten years in many cases. Before the data warehouse, applications stored a minimal amount of historical data, such as a week, month, or quarter.

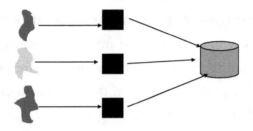

Figure 6-2. The data warehouse made data available for access and analysis.

A data warehouse is a:

- Subject oriented
- Integrated
- Non-volatile
- Time variant

collection of data for the purpose of management's decision-making.

A data warehouse is a "single version of the truth."

Data mart

A data mart customizes the data in the warehouse.

Figure 6-3. Marketing, sales, finance, and management needed their own versions of the data, and the data warehouse fed each of these data marts.

The dimensional model captures the structure of data marts. The source of data for the data marts was the data warehouse.

Data lakehouse

The origins of the data lakehouse lie in the need to prepare a bed of data for the data science community. The data scientist noticed a lot of data in the corporation besides transaction data. Among other things, machines produced analog data. And textual data appeared on the Internet, in emails, contracts, and elsewhere. The data scientist was interested in using that data to do a scientific investigation.

The analog data was fundamentally different from transaction data. Transaction data was filled with opportunities to find business value. Machine-generated data had much data for which there was no business value and some data with very high business value.

The different kinds of data in the data lakehouse are encompassed by an analytical infrastructure, making the data in the data lake accessible to the analytical and data science community. There were many parts to the analytical infrastructure, including:

- Description of tables, files, attributes, keys
- Identification of indexes
- Taxonomies
- Ontologies
- Data lineage
- Summarization information
- Selection/exclusion information
- Attribute definitions

The analytical infrastructure allowed the end user/data scientist to do many things, including connecting data from different environments. The strength of the connection between the different environments depends entirely on what connecting data there is that allows the different environments to be combined.

Once the data lakehouse is built along with the analytical infrastructure, analysts can perform analytical processing in the data lakehouse. In some cases, analysis occurs in the environments themselves. In other cases, processing data in a separate environment is more convenient. Moving data into a separate environment benefits the person doing heuristic analytical processing. In heuristic analytical processing, having a separate facility where data can be isolated from other data is often beneficial.

The data lakehouse can be placed on a single platform. But given the diversity of the data and its structure, it is often wise to have the different forms of data placed on physically separate structures.

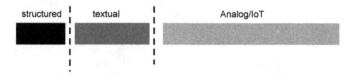

Figure 6-4. The data is so diverse and the day-to-day processing is so different that having separate platforms for the different kinds of data makes sense.

Comparing the data warehouse and the data lakehouse

The data warehouse and the data lakehouse have a great deal of similarities and at the same time have some distinct differences.

Some of the similarities between the data warehouse and the data lakehouse include:

- Data is included for analytical processing
- Data integrity is an important feature
- There is widespread usage of the data across the corporation
- The data is designed for end-user friendliness
- Both have their own analytical infrastructure
- Both contain historical data

In these regards, the data warehouse and the data lake are similar.

There are some distinctive differences between the environments:

- Data warehouse data is structured and transaction-based. Data lakehouse data includes all sorts of data
- Data warehouse data is processed by the record. Data lakehouse data is processed by the file
- Data warehouse data is normally subjected to regularly scheduled analytical processing, looking for the most recent Key Performance Indicator (KPI). Data lakehouse data does analysis heuristically
- Data warehouse data is designed for use by the data analyst. Data lakehouse data is designed for the data scientist

- The types of analysis done on data warehouse data are predictable. The results of processing data lakehouse are unpredictable
- The data warehouse makes use of data marts. The data lakehouse makes use of derived data
- The metadata found in the data warehouse is conspicuous. Conversely, the metadata found in the data lakehouse is inconspicuous

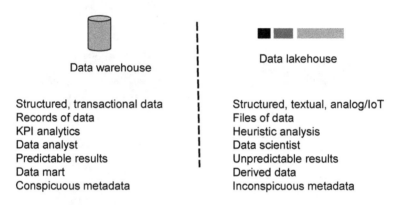

Data warehouse

Data lakehouse

Structured, transactional data
Records of data
KPI analytics
Data analyst
Predictable results
Data mart
Conspicuous metadata

Structured, textual, analog/IoT
Files of data
Heuristic analysis
Data scientist
Unpredictable results
Derived data
Inconspicuous metadata

Figure 6-5. The data warehouse and the data lakehouse have some very important differences.

CHAPTER 7

Dynamics of Data Lakehouse Processing

T he data lakehouse is architected to accommodate different types of data.

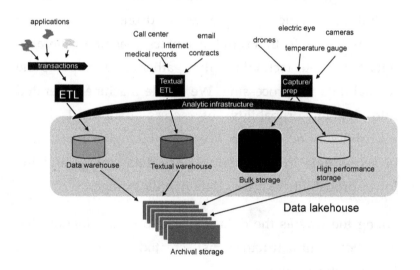

Figure 7-1. The data lakehouse is depicted in tan or light grey and contains structured, textual, and machine-generated data.

Data flowing into the data lakehouse

Applications are one of the sources of data for the data lakehouse. Therefore, application transactions go through ETL processing before arriving in the data warehouse.

Text comes from many places, including email, the Internet, corporate contracts, call centers, medical records, and more. From the textual sources, data flows into textual ETL. From textual ETL, data flows into a textual warehouse.

Machine-generated data comes from many sources, including electric eyes, cameras, drones, temperature gauges, and so forth. From the sources, machine-generated data flows into technology that gathers and prepares the textual data for processing. We divide machine-generated into higher probability of access data and lower probability of access data. We store the higher probability of access data in high-performance data storage and the lower probability of access data in bulk storage.

Along the way as the data is going to its destination, the analytical infrastructure is created. The analytical infrastructure includes:

- Table/database definition
- Source of data
- Lineage of data
- Selection inclusion/exclusion criteria

- Taxonomies
- Ontologies
- Data relationships
- Transformation rules

And so forth.

As long as the data remains useful, it stays in the lakehouse. As time passes and the value of the data diminishes, the data moves into archival storage.

At any moment, the data and the analytical infrastructure can change. A convenient way of thinking about that data lakehouse is that the data lakehouse is like a river. A river is constantly changing. The water that flows through the river is never the same, from one moment to the next.

Data scientist and the data architect

The data scientist wastes a lot of time wrestling with data. The organization, therefore, benefits by having the data scientist and the data architect split duties. When this split occurs, the data scientist spends less time wrestling data. It is much like a surgeon working with an anesthesiologist. When the surgeon knows that a competent anesthesiologist is working with him/her, the surgeon can focus on the surgery without worrying about the patient regaining consciousness during the operation.

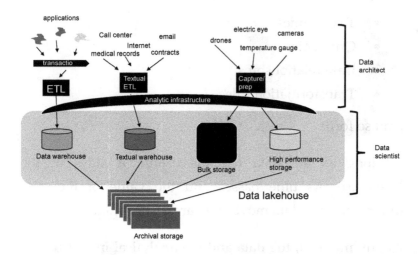

Figure 7-2. The proper domains of the data architect and the data
scientist.

Analytical sandbox

A convenient complement to the data lakehouse is the
analytical sandbox. The analytical sandbox is a collection
of data created to analyze some problem or trend. The data
in the sandbox is pulled from anywhere in the data
lakehouse that is appropriate.

The analytical sandbox is physically removed from the
data lakehouse. The analyst or data scientist uses the
analytical sandbox for analytical purposes. The data
analyst or the data scientist is free to do any kind of
analysis appropriate in the sandbox. For example, playing

with data and asking "what if" questions in the sandbox have no impact on the data found in the data lakehouse.

The only restriction is that operational decisions do not occur in the sandbox. That is because the data in the sandbox may have been artificial or incomplete. The sandbox can be archived or discarded at the end of the analysis.

The value of analysis in the sandbox is to test out ways to improve decision-making. Once we discover those ways, the process can be placed into the data lakehouse and run against actual data.

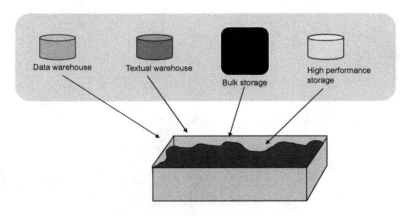

Figure 7-3. The sandbox represents a means for doing analytical processing in a non-disruptive manner.

The sandbox becomes the best place to do heuristic analytical processing.

CHAPTER 8

The Data Lakehouse Paradigm

Often we read "data warehouse *was*" and "data lake *was*" good for this or good for that, and "data lakehouse *is*" the best of both data warehouse and data lake. However, data warehouse and data lake are still part of the data lakehouse. The data lakehouse provides a fabric to leverage these technologies for all types of structured, text, and analog/IoT data.

Must be requirements-driven

Making textual business data accessible in the enterprise business decision-making process is challenging. Very few technologies have a level of capabilities to convert textual data to a structured format or alternative format for analysis. Unstructured data, including textual and analog/IoT data, requires preprocessing before it is part of the data lakehouse. For example, a scanned or printed document might need OCR processing, a voice recording might need transcription processing, and an image needs preprocessing to capture various parameters and metadata before being useful for analysis.

There can be many cases where understanding the business requirements and properly preparing unstructured data can add substantial business value. For example, a video used by the traffic police department may need to know who is violating or has violated the traffic rules. In contrast, a video for a movie censor board might be interested in analyzing if there are violence or obscene scenes in the movie so they can censor it for kids. Video streaming in a manufacturing unit or warehouse may want to see if the process is safe or if anyone on the shop floor is about to do a hazardous act. A chip fabricating and manufacturing company can use image processing intelligence to quality check the chips before fabrication or printing.

When to use what

A data warehouse is a good choice for companies seeking a mature, structured data solution that focuses on business intelligence and data analytics use cases. Data lakes are suitable for organizations seeking a flexible, low-cost, big-data solution to drive machine learning and data science workloads on unstructured data.

Suppose the data warehouse and data lake approaches aren't meeting your company's data demands, or you're looking for ways to implement both advanced analytics and machine learning workloads on your data. In that case, a data lakehouse is a reasonable choice.

Data lakehouses can be complex to build from scratch. And you'll most likely use a platform built to support an open data lakehouse architecture. So, carefully research each platform's different capabilities and implementations.

Whichever solution you choose, it should meet your enterprise business needs. It should continuously and non-intrusively ingest all your enterprise data from various sources in real-time for data warehousing. It should also preprocess your data in real-time as it is being delivered into the data lake stores to speed up downstream activities.

It all depends upon the need. You can even choose a data warehouse today and a data lakehouse tomorrow. Or build a data lakehouse on top of a data lake. There are many architectural options and approaches. It is similar to the approach to deciding whether and when to create a data mart after creating a data warehouse or vice versa.

The data warehouse, data lake, and data lakehouse can be prioritized, sequenced, or phased into an enterprise data platform different ways, depending on your business needs and what you would like to achieve.

A number of years ago, I was working with a financial company that wanted to build an enterprise data warehouse. I presented my approach and methodology to senior management, who communicated that although a full budget will be available shortly, their funds were extremely limited, and they could not implement the whole solution in the first pass.

The first way to save them money was to choose a bottom-up (application-driven) over a top-down (requirements-driven) approach. We would start with subject-oriented data marts and then consolidate to the ultimate enterprise data warehouse to meet the platform's final goal.

The various approaches and methodologies are very much situational.

Architectural paradigm

A data lakehouse is an analytical environment that can accommodate structured, semi-structured, and unstructured data. It enables business intelligence and machine learning operations easily, effectively, and efficiently.

A data lakehouse can provide intelligent metadata layers over unstructured data to the user to classify and categorize business data. Identifying and extracting features from the data allows for the capability to perform business analytics for various decision supports.

The data lakehouse architectural paradigm is a data management and implementation methodology using low-cost and directly-accessible storage. It provides traditional analytical RDBMS management and performance features such as ACID transactions, data versioning, auditing, indexing, caching, and query optimization.

Instead of creating a data lakehouse by building upon an existing data warehouse or data lake, you can use low-cost storage and create your own select intensive eco system for effective data management. Or you can use a vendor-provided solution to create your data lakehouse.

Data processing stages

First, we process for data quality. We clean, profile, massage, standardize, aggregate, anonymize, filter, and augment the data. Next, we process for analytics. Data enablement means making the data participate in business analytics. We must structure the large amount of semi-structured or textual data for analytics.

For example, we have work to do to make legal agreements, corporate contracts, textual medical history narrations, etc., useful for analytics. This includes managing all the different formats such as digital, hard copy, scanned images, videos, and voice recordings.

How can we analyze a hard copy of text like a legal agreement or contract? How can we use a textual PDF file for analytics? How can we analyze a doctor's medical statement? How can we compare two images of a national border taken a few months apart to see if there is any activity by a neighboring country? We need to pre-process all such data to make it analyzable.

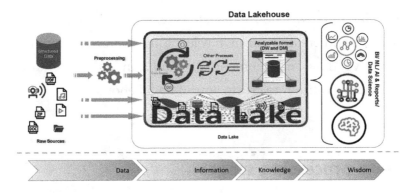

Figure 8-1. Data lakehouse reference architecture.

Strive to design a simple, versatile, open, and collaborative data lakehouse. Notice in the above data lakehouse architecture figure that the sources can be raw, including structured, semi-structured, and IoT device logs and text or any other form of unstructured data, including but not limited to video, audio, and images.

Those data sources may need pre-processing, including Optical Character Recognition (OCR), transcriptions, translations, and conversions, for better DSS (decision support system) for the respective business.

Data lakehouse data management and data governance can be more versatile if we accompany conventional data management and governance with modern Data Lakehouse Housekeeping™ methodologies, Data Future-proofing™, and successful implementation of FDM™ (Future-proof Data Management).

Analytical workbench

The data lakehouse is a paradigm that aims to give an enterprise a platform that can provide analysis for all types of data. More than the data warehouse, which only focuses on structured data. More than the data lake, which contains unstructured data, is not readily in a format for useful analytics.

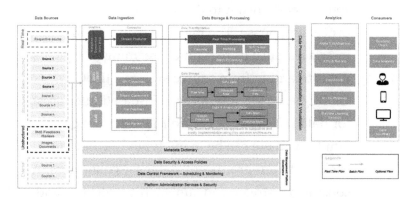

Figure 8-2. Data lakehouse analytical workbench architecture

We can create an analytical workbench in six phases:

1. **Data sourcing**. Data sourcing identifies, classifies, categorizes, and segregates heterogeneous and diversified source systems. We perform pre-processing needs analysis. We decide the usefulness of a set of data or the data source. We determine whether the effort required in its treatment is worth the value to the business. We determine if it is the only source for that specific data set or whether alternatives exist. Whether the given source is the primary source, secondary, or tertiary. We identify the reliability index of the source in question, and so forth. Data sources can be internal or external. Data sources can be at diversified locations across the globe.

2. **Data ingestion**. The data ingestion phase will have various types of interfaces and connectors to ingest the data from heterogeneous and diversified sources and push it to the data storage and processing phase. The ingestion can have many interfaces, such as real-time streaming to handle data streaming from source systems, JDBC- or ODBC-based DB interfaces, API-based interfaces for data ingestion, or secure FTP interfaces. Similarly, there can be many types of connectors, such as stream producers, database connectors, API consumers, stream consumers, file watchers, and file parsers.

3. **Data storage and processing**. Data storage and processing are the heart and soul of the overall analytical workbench. It is where we transform, process, and store. This is the phase where the data architect and data modeler determine the core data quality strategy and methodology to achieve the required data cleansing, profiling, and standardization. This is the phase where we model the target, map source to target, and write transformation logic. We perform business validation. We also consider Natural Language Processing (NLP) or textual ETL in this phase. We decide whether to use a top-down or bottom-up approach for data warehouse creation.

4. **Data analytics**. Data analytics is provisioned over and above the data storage done recently. We create Key Performance Indicator (KPI) reporting and dashboards, alerts and notifications, and Artificial Intelligence (AI) and Machine Learning (ML) pipelines during this phase. We can also create the Machine learning Sandbox if needed.

5. **Data consumption**. Data consumption by business users, data analysts, and data scientists can be through mobile or desktop. They are the consumers of the artifacts created in the data analytics phases.

6. **Data management and governance**. Here we focus on the metadata dictionary, which contains the

data access policy and data security. We consider controls like scheduling and monitoring in this phase. The whole workbench platform administration service and security is part of this phase.

The data transformation methodology is very subjective and based on business needs and use cases. For example, different business scenarios may lead to different ways of data ingestion. There can be a few cases where ETL is a best fit. In other cases, Extract, Load, and Transform (ELT) is the best method.

Let us discuss these two business scenarios to understand the needs of ETL versus ELT:

1. An airport authority looks after 100 domestic and international airports across the nation. Each airport has its own parking management system. The country's airport authority wants to tap the revenue leakage at various parking lots by creating a centralized data warehouse. There are over 100 sources and, therefore, doing transformations on the fly just after extraction and before load is not recommended. Transformation is needed after the data is loaded at the destination to reduce the risk of unnecessary carrier load and avoid any performance hit. The transformation after the load will be optimum performing and low cost in many ways. Hence we can easily recommend ELT.

2. A defense agency wanted completely new applications. They are on monolithic architecture and wanted a microservices architecture. Once they complete the new microservices architecture, the legacy data needs to be migrated to the new environment. Both legacy and new enterprise applications are in the same city and on the same network. So we can recommend ETL.

Deciding whether to go ETL or ELT is very much situational.

Data Lakehouse Housekeeping

Where there is a house, there is housekeeping. The first thing that comes to mind when we talk about a house is, "What does the house look like?" Then, you start imagining its exterior, interior, layout, design, aesthetics, lot size, connecting roads, architecture, and many more things a human can imagine about a house.

Once the house is built, you can't leave the house abandoned. An abandoned house starts looking like a haunted house after a few years or decades. Therefore, we need excellent housekeeping to maintain a beautifully built or constructed house. Housekeeping will keep the house maintained and in order by managing regular household affairs. Excellent and regular housekeeping will make the residents' stay in the house enjoyable, leading to the residents' happiness and delight year after year.

Housekeeping in terms of an organization means recordkeeping which facilitates productive work.

Similar is the case with a data lakehouse. We need to set up the housekeeping processes in place for a data lakehouse to be a data lakehouse forever, or else it becomes a data lake (like a haunted house in the above example). "Data Lakehouse Housekeeping" will help keep the data lakehouse in order year over year.

Data lakehouse housekeeping helps maintain and keep the data lakehouse in order year over year.

Please remember that the housekeeping process establishes the strong distinction between a data lake and data lakehouse. As we know, a data lakehouse brings in the best of both data warehouse and data lake. It helps you maintain the hygiene of the lakehouse. This housekeeping will help the data lakehouse maintain its identity year over year and not become a data swamp or a data lake.

It is the process of housekeeping that can help you establish a data lakehouse from a data lake.

The housekeeping of the data lakehouse will help maintain the standard data acquisition, transformation, federation, and extraction processes. It also helps regulate data management and governance in the lakehouse.

Data lakehouse housekeeping will make a data lakehouse a data lakehouse—else it is simply a data lake.

Once you think of a data lakehouse, what kind of housekeeping can keep the data lakehouse in order? Is it by managing all data-related household affairs within the lakehouse? In terms of data lakehouse housekeeping, examples of questions to address are:

- How will the data be integrated within the data lakehouse?
- How interoperable should it be?
- How can we manage the master reference within the data lakehouse?
- How can we manage the single version of the truth?
- What privacy and confidentiality measures need to be considered and applied within the data lakehouse?
- How can we make sure that the data is relevant and usable, even decades in the future?
- How do we do data lakehouse routine maintenance?

A data lakehouse without data lakehouse housekeeping is only the data lake. We dump the source data as is by following standard data lake creation processes.

To combine a data warehouse's robustness with a data lake's capabilities into a data lakehouse, we need disciplined and meticulous data lakehouse housekeeping.

Data integration and interoperability

Data integration and data interoperability include:

- Data acquisition
- Data extraction
- Data transformation
- Data movement
- Data replication
- Data federation

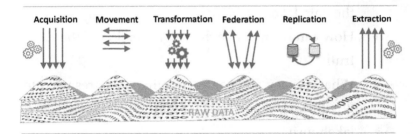

Figure 9-1. Aspects of data integration and data interoperability in a data lakehouse.

Data acquisition

Data acquisition includes but is not limited to converting the physical condition of data into a digital and structured form for further storage and analysis. Typically, IoT data also includes signals from sensors, voice, text, Textual ETL outputs, logs, and many more sources. A data lakehouse is designed to store IoT data. After acquisition, the transformation is optional and subject to format differences before dumping the data into the data lakehouse.

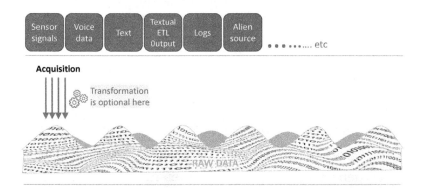

Figure 9-2. Data Acquisition from heterogeneous sources in a data lakehouse.

Data extraction

Data extraction is the first step in any data ingestion process.

Data extraction is the process of extracting data from databases or software as a service platform, including any architecture pattern like the data lake or data lakehouse.

The extraction happens in both directions. After acquiring the data, you extract the source data to the data lake. And there are lots of architectural patterns that need to be applied to call that data lake a data lakehouse. We can then extract data from the data lakehouse for various consumption purposes.

Data extraction is the first step in the data ingestion process.
The data ingestion process can be either ETL or ELT. 'Extract'
is the first step in both processes.

Data transformation

Data transformation is the process of mapping and converting data from one format to another. Data transformation is needed when you expect data from heterogeneous sources due to different data formats from across sources. This transformed format is nothing but the uniform format decided for the data lakehouse. Data transformation is a component of almost all data integration and management activities, including data warehousing and data lakehouse creation.

Data transformation takes place in almost all data integration
and data management activities.

Data transformation is needed in a data lakehouse when integrating heterogeneous sources like XML, XLS, Word, text, PDF, RDBMS, textual ETL outputs, CSVs, and flat files. Transformation can also be for bidirectional purposes, including inbound and outbound from the data lake. Transformation is even required internally as well when it comes to data lakehouse formation, because data lakehouse frameworks transform the data from the data lake. Transformation is needed when the data needs to be mapped due to data format differences or source-to-destination file or format differences. In s few cases, it might be simple and straightforward. In another case, it might be complex, requiring potential changes to the data and its format before it reaches the destination file or storage format and is stored for successful hassle-free uses.

Transformation is needed whenever and wherever there are format differences, and the data between source and destination needs a strategic mapping with appropriate transformation rules.

Three things are important to decide whether the data needs any transformation before storing it in the target file format. First is the source data format understanding, second is the desired data format expected into the destination, and third is the transformation logic to be applied to bring the difference to an acceptable format into the final destination file and storage data format.

Master references for the data lakehouse

Why master references in a data lakehouse? A data lakehouse is not a data lake. In a data lake, you might not need a master reference. But as we have learned, a data lakehouse is the best of both data warehouse and data lake. Hence, a managed master reference becomes obvious. A master reference is the reference of master data to manage shared data to reduce redundancy and ensure better data quality through standardized definition and data values. It helps maintain a single version of the truth across systems.

> *A distinction between shared and distinct data across the organization is very important in data lakehouse housekeeping. It helps you build the master reference.*

Figure 9-3. The master reference layer in a data lakehouse.

Earmarking such shared data will help maintain a single version of the truth across the data lakehouse. A data lakehouse is not the dumping yard. At one end, it will store data from heterogeneous sources. At another end, it will be the source of truth for various external but dependent systems. Various enterprise systems might extract required data periodically or regularly from the data lakehouse. In some cases, the data lakehouse might be the direct source of data for a few enterprise applications, including but not limited to various analytics, data science, or cognitive tools/applications.

The data lakehouse can be a source of truth for various external systems within or outside an enterprise.

Once master reference earmarking is over, the layer needs to be structured and brought into use. Every system or segment of data within and outside the data lakehouse (consumers of data lakehouse) should rely only on the reference and master data designed for the purpose. It must be part of all ETL happening over the data lakehouse.

Next comes the question of precedence of references for master data. This is a very natural question and it has solutions already existing and used almost everywhere to create any master information repository. Product owners or functional experts decide the precedence of data to overwrite and/or update a data into reference data or the master data store. And application engineers need to write the rule engine that needs to be followed for any master data overwrite/update or even delete (a soft or physical delete).

For example, an enterprise has many applications that capture a customer's address. It might be captured in a CRM, a sales application, and a finance or billing application. All applications might have captured the same customer's address differently. For example, the CRM might have captured its customer's address as 'Sector – 53, Gurgaon, India.' The sales application might have an older address from this same customer, 'Chanakyapuri, New Delhi.' But today, this customer is staying in 'Bangalore, India,' and the billing has the latest updated address.

So, once an enterprise has a master reference, all applications will rely upon that single version of truth. And for the first creation of that single version of the truth, the precedence rule needs to be written that says which address will go and sit in the master reference. And here in this example, the billing application address should be the most current.

Data lakehouse privacy, confidentiality, and data protection

Data privacy, data confidentiality, and data protection are sometimes incorrectly diluted with security.

For example, data privacy is related to, but not the same as, data security. Data security is concerned with assuring data confidentiality, integrity, and availability. Data privacy focuses on how and to what extent businesses may collect and process information about individuals.

You can say that privacy needs security (there is no privacy without security), but security doesn't need privacy. A data lakehouse must maintain data privacy and data confidentiality with data protection.

Data privacy, interchangeably called information privacy, often refers to a specific kind of privacy linked to personal information provided to private actors in various contexts. Here the definition of personal information is very subjective and may be defined differently in different contexts and domains. For example, personal information on social media might be your personal credentials, including name, sex, age, address, contact number, ethnicity, and so on. Personal information in healthcare might include vital EMR attributes like diagnosis, health conditions, vitals, treatments, and so on.

Data confidentiality deals with protecting against the disclosure of information by ensuring that the data is limited to those authorized, or by representing the data in such a way that its actual or original value remain accessible only to those who are entitled or possess some critical information (e.g. a decryption or decoding key for an encrypted or coded data).

For example, a patient was diagnosed with AIDS. But the patient might not be interested in sharing his/her medical condition or the diagnosis of AIDS to anyone except his/her doctor who is treating him/her. Hence it is the hospital's accountability to maintain the confidentiality of the data of that specific patient. The application used to capture and store his/her data should be capable of handling this confidentiality. These data confidentiality rules apply to the data lake or data lakehouse where that data ultimately resides.

Data protection is the process of safeguarding important data or information from corruption, compromise, or loss. The definition of *importance* can be different for different entities or organizations. Important data can be unpublished financial information, customer data, patents, formulas or new proprietary technologies, pricing strategies, etc. Hence, the data protection process should be robust enough and comprehensive enough to address all such required data protection to defined enterprise data.

A few commonly known data or information privacy, confidentiality, and protection policies are:

- The Health Insurance Portability and Accountability Act (HIPAA)
- The Family Educational Rights and Privacy Act (FERPA)
- The Children's Online Privacy Protection Act (COPPA)
- The Gramm-Leach-Bliley Act (GLBA)
- The European Union's General Data Protection Regulation (GDPR)
- The California Consumer Privacy Act (CCPA)

When you do the housekeeping of a data lakehouse, have a data protection process for privacy policies, applicable confidentiality rules, and regulations. As mentioned, it is very subjective and may be defined differently in different contexts. Act responsibly while dealing with data privacy and confidentiality in a data lakehouse architecture pattern. Remember that a data lakehouse is very much part of the enterprise system. The data privacy, confidentiality, and data protection rules should be more comprehensively applied to a data lake or data lakehouse because a data lakehouse will accommodate data from hundreds or thousands of applications.

While housekeeping a data lakehouse, awareness of the applicable data privacy and confidentiality rules and a robust data protection process is essential.

"Data future-proofing™" in a data lakehouse

In terms of data, 'future-proofing' can be defined as the process of anticipating the future and developing methods of capturing and arranging the data in a way that can minimize the gap due to missing data or irrelevant data, for the future purpose of relevant data driven researches, correlations, trends, patterns, data supported evidences, past incidents, and many more. It can give you the confidence to prove and support your past data findings and help reduce unwanted shocks and surprises that can cause business stress due to missing future-proof data.

All data of an enterprise might not be relevant for that enterprise 10-20 or 50 years later. Organizational stakeholders within an enterprise must coordinate with data architects to decide and earmark core entities and attributes relevant and useful for the business benefits even in the far future.

> *"Data Future Proofing" is a new phrase and is the process of anticipating the future and developing methods of capturing and arranging the data in a way that can minimize the gap due to missing data or relevant data for the purpose of relevance, data-driven researches, correlations, trends, patterns, data-supported evidences, past incidents, and experiences.*

We should not forget the importance of a data lakehouse for an enterprise. It is meant for the long term. Technology will keep evolving, employees, consultants, and vendors may come and go within an enterprise, but accumulated data relevance will always be there for an enterprise. Next-gen business is all about data. All cognitive activities (including cognitive science) revolve around the data you accumulate, whether healthcare-related or insurance.

Aviation data, environmental, or weather data. Social, socio-economic data, or behavioral data. Geographical, political, or geopolitical data. Space data or the research data of any field of study. More past data or proven historical data can help in better future findings. Because, "Data is the New Gold."

Technology will keep evolving, organizations will keep changing, but accumulated data relevance will always be there for an enterprise.

The most important question is, "Which data needs to be preserved, accumulated, stored, and saved for future purposes?" We think a few years ahead when creating a data warehouse or data lake. It was never considered for decades or centuries. Here we consider the importance of data till eternity that can be passed from generation to generation. But we should be sensitive about its significance and relevance. We can't consider all gathered enterprise data as future-proof data. All data might not retain its relevance in the future. It will be a silly consideration and may lead to various problems, including but not limited to size, volume, policy breaches, and misinterpretations or misuses at later stages.

Future proof data should be capable of fulfilling any past data needs for various analytics and research purposes.

While considering future-proofing of data, we need to be sensitive about various aspects of data, including its relevance, relevant grain level, context, format, dimensions for different perspectives, future views, and viewpoints.

In this data context, a data view is what data you see and a data viewpoint is where you are looking from. Data viewpoints are a means to focus on the business data for particular aspects of the business. These aspects are determined by the concerns or business purposes with whom communication occurs to future-proof the data. Remember, the data viewpoints may sometimes depend upon the stakeholder's perspective and may be subjective. Be a little generic while deciding the prospective candidates (which subjects, entities, and attributes to capture) for future data-proofing. A little generic does not mean 'taking everything' because being more generic may capture data that may not be useful in the future and spoil the purpose of "Data Future Proofing."

Figure 9-4. Two different views of the same subject from two different viewpoints.

> *Data viewpoints are determined based on the business concerns and generally created in coordination with the core stakeholders.*

Think about medical records. Capturing medical records is important. What are the value and benefits of historical medical records? What benefits does it bring to healthcare if utilized efficiently and effectively? Yes, it can help save human life. It can help in early diagnosis. It can help in medical research in many ways. It can help with faster vaccine creation for deadly health-related threats. It has the potential to reduce healthcare stress by many fold.

Take even the COVID pandemic scenario. If future-proofing would have been done for all the past medical records of similar epidemics or pandemics like Ebola, Avian Influenza, Mers, and H1N1, today's scenarios would have been far better.

But do you know how much privacy and confidentiality clauses a medical record carries? Handling medical records is a sensitive subject. Storing medical records at the application level is different than storing them in a data warehouse, data lake, or data lakehouse. When you bring a medical record to your data lakehouse, the purpose is not to treat a specific patient. Instead, the organization might utilize the medical records in the data lakehouse for various medical research purposes, early diagnosis, accurate treatment, preventive healthcare, and so forth.

Medical research, early diagnosis, proven treatment findings, or preventive healthcare methodology findings, do not require knowing the patient's name and Social Security Number. For example, do you really need the phone number of a patient diagnosed with the influenza virus in 1968 and was treated in a city hospital? You might need the age (or age group), sex, city/state, and certainly the medical conditions, including the symptoms, dates, diagnosis, treatment, and the result of that treatment.

Another very common scenario where data future-proofing can help from data vulnerability is an enterprise that captures personal and sensitive data. Personal data like name, address, medical details, and bank details and sensitive data like racial information, political opinion, religion, trade union association information, health, sex life, and criminal activity. The enterprise has been doing its business for more than two decades. Then the company is acquired by another business house from a different domain or sector, such as a retail company acquired a software development company or a manufacturing company acquired a marketing research company. What will be the future of the personal and sensitive data captured by the first enterprise if data future-proofing was not done? There are chances of accidental exposure to those tons of personal and sensitive data kept by the previous organization. You never know if the new owning organization has the support to handle such data.

Data future-proofing can help reduce the data vulnerability risks for an enterprise.

Now let us discuss how data future-proofing is done. We have divided data future-proofing processes into five different phases—Identification, Elimination, Future-proofing, Organization, and Storage.

Five phases of "Data Future-proofing"

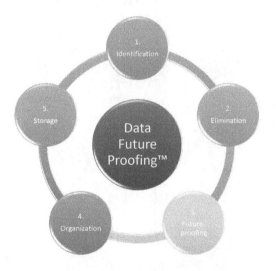

Figure 9-5. Five phases of data future-proofing.

Identification phase

Keeping the purpose of the future data in your mind (such as for analytics and research), identify all entities and attributes relevant and meaningful for various business needs and benefits. You need to identify only those future-proof entities and attributes of your business domain, such as healthcare, insurance, aviation, manufacturing, education, transportation, hospitality, and retail.

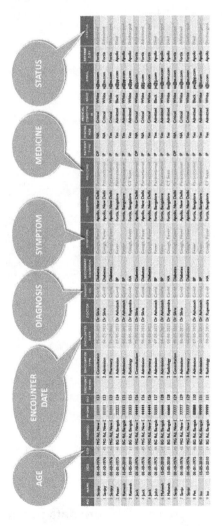

Figure 9-6. How to identify future-proof data and attributes.

For example, the EMR might have hundreds of attributes in a healthcare domain, but you might need very few of them. The grain level of an EMR is up to every patient encounter. Still, for the future, you might need the extraction level from the disease, number of patients diagnosed with that disease, their gender, age group, cure status, and ultimate treatment.

The main purpose for future-proofing the data is to help execute analytics and research work.

Elimination phase

Eliminate all those entities and attributes without significance for future analysis or research. For example, eliminate sensitive, future sensitive, future proof, and controversial data. Follow an elimination method to be more specific—it helps narrow down data easily and quickly. For example, how important is it to capture the shoe quantity a customer bought per order in the retail domain? Instead, we should focus on the type, color, or design of the shoes trending during every decade and what kind of shoes are trending today. This may give a perspective on fashion trends over time. This requires capturing information like shoe types, brands, periods, number of pairs sold, and so on. For example, EMR data from the healthcare domain is on the facing page. We had shown the future-proof data sets earlier. There are other types of data, like personal, sensitive, and controversial.

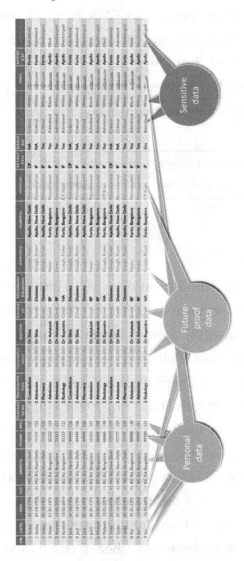

Figure 9-7. Personal, future proof, and sensitive data. Personal, future proof, and sensitive data are shown in blue and red color respectively.

Eliminate sensitive, future-sensitive, and controversial data while preparing your future-proof data sets.

You can understand that attributes are sensitive only if they are supported and served with personal data. For example, a patient's medical condition and diagnosis can be sensitive if supported and linked to personal information like Social Security Number. Similarly, the patient's race can only come under the controversial category of data if it is linked to the specific patient through an identifier or name.

In general, a data or data set contains its sensitivity or controversial nature only if it is linked or related to an individual's personal information. Else an isolated, abandoned, or unrelated sensitive or controversial attribute has no significance.

Future-proofing phase

By following phases 1 and 2, you have completed half of the future-proofing job. You identified only the data that will have relevance in the future. You eliminated all sensitive and controversial personal data. In addition, if you have data you think might not be fair to expose for future use, or that it might be misleading, or bias any data analysis once exposed for future business purposes, you should anonymize it. Data to be concerned about is (a) personal data like name, address, medical details, and banking details and (b) sensitive data, like racial or ethnic origin, political opinions, religion, membership of a trade union, health, sex life, and criminal activity.

With data anonymization, you retain the purpose yet you don't expose the actual data.

These two categories of data might create biased decisions or may create controversies in the future. Especially category '(b)' is more sensitive for political subjects. Hence data anonymization will be a handy tool for this purpose.

Once you notice that a potentially sensitive or controversial attribute will be part of a future-proof data set, anonymize the associated personal information.

In most business scenarios, we do not need a detailed level or the lowest grain level of data for future use. The lowest level data is generally required in a transactional environment. Hence, we should judiciously decide the grain level of data while future-proofing your data. Deciding the required grain is a very important aspect while future-proofing the data. This will decide the volume of your future-proof data every year or decade.

> *The more data is aggregated, the less the chance of personal and sensitive data vulnerability.*

Data in its lowest grain level are the raw form of records that may incorporate personal and sensitive data that are more vulnerable if not handled responsibly.

A data lake or data lakehouse can contain the lowest grain level of data. Hence, we need to be more sensible and preferably give priority to the data future-proofing features.

> *In principle, isolated, abandoned, or unrelatable sensitive or controversial attributes can be part of future-proof data because it has no significance until it is linked back to a person, place, or thing.*

In a healthcare data use case, 50 years from now, one might not be interested in knowing whether 'Mr. Sanjay' (name) from 'New Delhi' (location/address) was a 'Hindu' (religion) and had COVID, and if he had, what was his CRT value? It might not solve any industrial problem, and it might not address any business issues at that time. Rather it might trigger some sensitive political issues or might fulfill biased interest. But suppose COVID or a similar type of virus resurfaces in 50 years. In that case, the healthcare industry might be interested in knowing the percentage of COVID-positive patients between 40-50 years of age and their average CRT value? What was the overall mortality rate? What were the recovery rates for the different age groups of people? Which medicine or drug showed the best results during its treatment? What were the infection spread ratios between males, females, and kids?

And such information requirements and fulfillment will address lots of business problems at that time. It may help healthcare professionals solve lots of healthcare issues. It may save many human lives. So, it is evident that we may not have any reason to store data with the lowest grain level.

Future-proofing of data can help you eliminate unnecessary data burden, reduce storage, reduce data vulnerability and minimize enterprise data complexity.

The next important part of future-proofing is to future-proof the data capture cycle. Once you have decided the grain level and extraction level, you can write extraction rules, and then based on the capture cycle, capture your future-proof data. Your capture cycle can be daily, monthly, quarterly, or yearly. The mode of capture should be any supported storage mode, depending upon your destination system of storage. In this case, your data lakehouse supported mode will be your mode of storage.

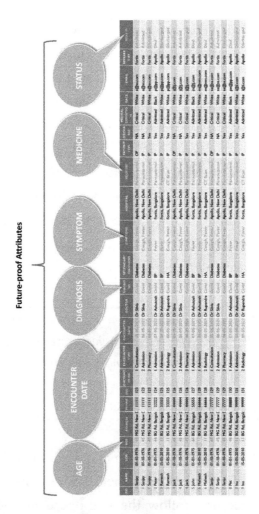

Figure 9-8. Future proof attributes in an EMR data set.

Organization phase

Unlike your conventional organization of data into the destination system and any special data management organization such as MDM or CDM, we propose having a separate **FDM™** (Future-proof Data Management) layer in your destination data management, in this case, in the data lakehouse. A separate data layer can also be proposed for the FDM if required. Please remember that FDM has nothing to do with MDM and CDM design or architecture. As MDM and CDM help manage enterprise data efficiently, FDM will help future-proof data be treated specially for future business benefits efficiently and strategically. So, this FDM layer should be treated special and designed by following the five phases of data future-proofing discussed in this section.

FDM is an implementation of an enterprise-wide system where the organization accesses its historical information for any future use from a single managed place. A central repository is created and all requests for future-proof data are satisfied from that one point.

The creation of an FDM system is not very complex. It is a repository of past business facts and figures. Keep the design simple and follow the five-phase process of data future-proofing.

FDM or future-proof data management allows the business to get their historical information at a single managed place for future purposes. A central future-proof data repository is created, and all requests related to future-proof data are satisfied from that one point.

Figure 9-9. The FDM (Future-proof Data Management) layer with a
data lakehouse.

Storage phase

Once it comes to the storage of FDM (Future-proof Data
Management), use an open format, generic platform-based
system because data future-proofing is for the long term.
Hence a proprietary or vendor-locked format or platform
will not meet the overall purpose of data future-proofing.

> *Most of the data lakehouse platforms support an open storage
> format consistent with the FDM's basic requirements.*

In this phase, you must ascertain the **accessibility** of the
future-proof data sets. Who should have access to the data
and permission to insert, update, and delete any data in
FDM should be decided and ascertained in this phase only.

We must also determine the availability of the FDM. It is
the nature of the FDM that it does not fall under 99.99999%
availability requirement category. But yes, it should be
available for any future use. The future can even be the
next year of your business because this year's data is past
data for you for next year.

Once you have ascertained accessibility and availability, storage upgradation is the last but not the least important strategy under this storage phase. Ensure the storage upgradation is done for the FDM where you have kept all your future-proof data to be accessed seamlessly using the latest storage platform year after year and decade after decade. Remember, data future-proofing is for eternity or until your business no longer exists.

Data lakehouse routine maintenance

The data lakehouse maintenance cycle is part of data lakehouse housekeeping.

Most data lakehouse platforms are self-maintained, and their framework has robust data governance and data management methodologies. But still, as part of data lakehouse housekeeping, we should use these data lakehouse maintenance steps to keep the lakehouse in order year after year.

The secret of data lakehouse maintenance is in its successful implementation. We should automate most of the processes using the provided utilities or tools into a data lakehouse platform.

Figure 9-10. The data lakehouse routine maintenance lifecycle.

Meticulous planning and design of a data lakehouse supported with robust data lakehouse housekeeping, will lead to a great business benefit to the enterprise.

CHAPTER 10

FDM in Data Lakehouse

Future-proof Data Management (FDM) is an innovative discipline in which the business and technology think together to preserve the past for the future. We propose to have a separate FDM layer in the data lakehouse. The FDM has nothing to do with Master Data Management (MDM). MDM helps manage enterprise data efficiently, whereas FDM ensures the future business benefits of data efficiently and strategically. MDM is helpful when the enterprise holds more than one copy of the data about a business entity. Similarly, FDM will help the business manage their data that is future-proof. That helps the business refer to the FDM for their past needs for many types of business analysis, including but not limited to trend analysis and AI- and ML-based analytics for various decision supports.

FDM process

So, we should treat the FDM layer as special and designed by following all five phases of Data Future Proofing discussed in the previous chapter.

FDM is an implementation of an enterprise-wide system where businesses get their historical information for any future use from a single managed place. We create a central repository and all requests for future-proof data are satisfied from that one managed source.

Creating an FDM system is not very complex. It is a repository of past business facts and figures. Keep the design simple and follow the data future-proofing process covered in the last chapter.

Figure 10-1. FDM (Future-proof Data Management) layer with a data lakehouse.

Once it comes to FDM storage, we recommend an open format, generic platform-based system, vendor-independent infrastructure with no proprietary format storage. This is because data future-proofing is for the long term—a proprietary or vendor-locked format will not last generations. Most of the data lakehouse platforms support open format of storage that is in line with the basic requirements of the FDM.

Next, we need to ascertain the accessibility of the future-proof data sets. Who should have access to the data and who can have permission to insert, update, and delete any data in FDM?

Next, we discuss the availability of the FDM. The FDM does not need to be 100% available.

Once you have ascertained accessibility and availability, storage upgradation is the last but not the least important strategy under this storage phase. Make sure the storage upgradation is done for the FDM where you have kept all your future-proof data so that it can be accessed seamlessly using the latest storage platform year over year and decade over decade. Remember, data future-proofing as long as your organization or industry exist.

The data lakehouse might use intelligent metadata layers that act as an intermediary between the unstructured data and the user to classify the data into different categories. By identifying and extracting features from the data, we can structure it effectively, allowing it to be cataloged and indexed just as if it was analyzable and tidy structured data.

Modeling strategy

A data model helps organize elements of data. Following and applying formal techniques establishes a special relationship among those different data elements. We have heard many data modeling myths around the data lakehouse. We know that a data lakehouse is the best of both data warehouse and data lake. Do we model for the data warehouse and data lake?

Yes! However, the nature of data modeling can be different in different cases.

For example, a data warehouse might need a dimensional modeling approach for a select intensive Online analytical processing (OLAP) application. Dimensional modeling is used to create star schemas and snowflake designs.

The Operational Data Store (ODS) might need to be normalized and follow the Entity-Relationship (ER) modeling approach to cater to its respective purpose. ER represents the relationships between entities in a database through formal diagrams. Multiple tools and techniques exist to create ER data model visuals that can convey database design objectives. ER modeling doesn't require a detailed understanding of the data storage's physical properties. In it, data segments are explicitly joined through tables, reducing database complexity.

A data lake can accommodate structured as well as unstructured data. Hence the data modeling required is also diverse, including but not limited to file system, object-based design, ER, and dimensional modeling. We can model file systems with a hierarchical structure, where each record has a single root or parent, which maps to one or more child tables through one-to-many relationships.

With object-oriented data modeling, the "objects" involved are abstractions of real-world entities. Objects are grouped in class hierarchies and have associated features. Object-oriented databases can incorporate tables and support more complex data relationships.

So the ultimate point here is that the data lakehouse is the best of both worlds and these worlds need data modeling. However, we must note that the data lakehouse doesn't only contain structured data. Therefore, multiple modeling techniques are required.

Normalization and Denormalization

Normalization means that all of the data elements are properly organized into sets and connected to other sets through relationships. A denormalized data model is not the same as a data model that has not been normalized. Denormalization should only occur after a satisfactory level of normalization has occurred and any required constraints have been created to deal with the inherent anomalies in the design. Examples of denormalization include flattened tables, star schemas, and OLAP cubes.

Factors deciding whether to denormalize include the type of relationship (e.g. one-to-many versus many-to-many), entities containing very few data elements, and entities used often in queries. Denormalization allows us to represent data in multiple ways to speed up queries without introducing inconsistencies. Denormalization can resolve performance problems, simplify complex structures, and aid reporting applications.

Design strategy

Readily accessible data storage format

We recommend designing the FDM in a readily accessible data storage format. We need to be ready to actively participate in the relevant business analytics at any time in the future by avoiding vendor lock-in. A format that most of the analytics or visualization tools accept directly without further transformation of the format of the data. csv, parquet, and many such file formats are universally accepted by most analytics and visualization tools. They are convenient for AI- and ML-based advanced analytics too.

No vendor lock-in

Avoid any vendor lock-in-based products to store the FDM and FDM-related data. Avoid getting into the vendor lock-in by using any COTS (commercially of the shelf) product or other means. The FDM being the reference data for future usage, any such kind of lock-in can be fatal and costly. You never know which vendor will go out of business or product become obsolete.

Autopilot design

We need to design the FDM so that it is self-contained and maintained. Due to its transactional nature, maintenance overhead might be acceptable for current business data. However, it can be a show-stopper for the business and can have a further funding challenge. We don't want any such hurdle that hampers the accumulation and ingestion of FDM. Any such break or unwanted interval in FDM data will spoil the FDM's purpose. Autopilot means the sources and targets are pre-defined, extraction level and transformation logics are pre-written, jobs and trigger points are pre-set—there are minimal manual interventions.

Avoid multiple versions

Avoid multiple versions of the same type of data in the FDM, unless it is obvious and mandatory to have more than one version of a similar attribute or set of attributes. We recommend that all the versions be handled together regarding the associated data operations if multiple versions are required.

Implementation strategy

We highly recommend implementing the FDM centrally and enterprise-wide for better results and to avoid any data redundancy and conflicting data within the FDM layer.

Create a strategy and roadmap to answer these questions to help yourself while designing the FDM layer for your enterprise:

- What do you want to achieve?
- Which tasks can help you achieve it?
- How should we sequence these tasks?
- What benefits will you get out of it and when?
- How much is it going to cost?

The purpose can be:

- Facilitating future decision support
- Performing research, like market research, healthcare, and medical research
- Applying analytics, including statistical analysis, trend analysis, future projection, and roadmap creation
- Learning about the business from past data

Tasks can be:

- Relevant and future proof entity and attribute identification

- Anonymization (if required)
- Ingestion
- Transformation (if needed)
- Data Quality
- Storage and preservation in future-proof formats

Order is situational and completely based on business needs. Transformation might come during ingestion or after ingestion. Data quality task positioning is situational and sometimes taken care of at the source or the destination.

In most business cases, we eliminate personally identifiable and sensitive data while we design the FDM. And in case we need to maintain those attributes for future use, we recommend applying anonymization for data privacy purposes due to the risk of sensitive data exposure or the cost of applying data security.

Benefits can be:

- Reduced business liability over historical data
- Reduced storage due to elimination of personal and other sensitive data
- Reduced cost of storage in the cloud or on premise
- Reduced cost of data security
- Faster retrieval by keeping and maintaining readily accessible data format

Cost can be:

- One time design cost
- Storage cost
- Maintenance cost

FDM as a business mandate

We must issue the FDM as a business mandate for its successful implementation and execution. We envision that it becomes required for every organization for the betterment and ease of the future of the business and associated research and analysis. And to reach that level, we must convey and discuss the benefits of the FDM to the decision-makers. We should openly discuss the FDM's financial and business benefits and futuristic nature.

We need to communicate that if we don't implement the FDM, how the unnecessary and avoidable cost overheads can impact the enterprise bottom line and how we will end up wasting funds on large volume data storage for any future use. We can't afford to let the FDM's purpose dilute due to a change in management or other administrative or policy reason. It should not fall to the mercy of an executive. If this happens, the FDM will not cater to the enterprise's future data needs.

Today organizations are not only growing organically. Inorganic growth is quite rampant. In fact, such a model of growth is working wonderfully for many enterprises that want faster growth and easy market coverage. The moment it comes to inorganic growth, the following factors become the root cause for data future-proofing:

- Business unit bifurcation or separation
- Product line segmentation
- Merger
- Acquisitions
- Change in management
- Change in policies
- Change in business priorities

All these above factors can impact your data accumulation for the future. Therefore, it becomes tricky to manage such data considering these factors can impact the process directly or indirectly. Hence the FDM layer across the organization can address and mitigate such challenges.

CHAPTER 11

Leveraging Data Effectively in the Data Lakehouse

The data lakehouse paradigm was born due to certain limitations in the existing data lake architecture. The challenge was how to leverage enterprise data effectively for the betterment of the organization.

People learned to ingest, stream, transform, load, design, and optimize structured data in a data warehouse. But what to do with all that unstructured data that can offer business value? Put it in a data lake. However, just dumping unstructured data into a data lake loses context, and slowly that data lake became a data swamp.

Figure 11-1. Data lakehouse architecture.

Then data professionals created the data lakehouse to produce business value from both structured and unstructured data. They also devised a method to capture metadata for unstructured data through intelligent metadata layers.

Data storage

Having a data storage strategy can:

- **Reduce cost**. The cost of storing data in the data lake, data warehouse, staging, or ODS can get expensive. Costs depend upon the nature of the data and the business tolerance of retrieval time. For example, if an organization can afford a retrieval latency of a few hours for data over two years old, this data can be stored in cold storage and the cost will be extremely low. However, if the data needs to be retrieved in near real time, this data will need to be stored in hot storage.

- **Ease maintenance.** If data is in hot storage, the storage maintainability will be high. The cold will have respectively low or no maintainability. Cold storage is designed for low maintainability.

- **Increase performance.** The storage decision impacts the acceptable latency or response time of a process or data retrieval time. For example, an airport authority maintaining the centralized data lakehouse of a eVPMS (electronic vehicle parking management system) might not be interested in looking at the previous year's parking data at its lowest grain level. In such a case, a proposal of pushing data older than one year to cold storage is fair enough. At the same time, only the current year's data should be in hot storage, saving tons of revenue for the enterprise.

- **Avoid lock-in.** A data lakehouse is for the long term, so ensure there is no vendor lock-in on data storage.

- **Increase compatibility with other tools and technologies.** We need to confirm any selected tool, technology, or platform for its compatibility to other associated tools and technologies. With technology continuously evolving, such due diligence will help the organization long term.

So storage can be cold, warm, or hot:

Type of	Property		Availability	
Storage	Cost	Time to retrieve	Cloud	On-premise
Cold	Low	Slow	Yes	Yes
Warm	Medium	Moderate	Yes	Yes
Hot	High	Fast	Yes	Yes

Cloud versus non-cloud

So whether it is a cloud environment or non-cloud environment of the underlying data lakehouse, it should solve the purpose of the underlying business. We should note that the data lakehouse paradigm applies in both cloud and non-cloud environments.

When it comes to cloud, we can think of private, public, or virtual private cloud. On-premise can be as per the enterprise architecture.

Microservices

Modernization may also include decomposing a monolith application into a set of independently developed, deployed, and managed microservices. The decoupled nature of a microservices environment allows each service to evolve in an agile and independent way. While there are many benefits for moving to a microservices-based architecture, there are also tradeoffs. As your monolithic application evolves into independent microservices, you must consider the implications to your data architecture.

A lakehouse architecture embraces the decentralized nature of microservices by facilitating data movement. These transfers of data can be:

- Source systems to data store like staging or ODS
- Between data stores
- From data store to data lake or vice versa
- From data lake to data warehouse
- From MDM to other data stores like the data lake, ODS, or data warehouse, or vice versa
- From data store to external systems

A microservices architecture-based development containing the following features offers great value:

Containerized
- Loosely coupled
- Convenient Agile development
- Ease in Continuous Integration and Continuous Delivery (CICD)
- Highly secure
- Environmental consistency

A microservices architecture is loosely coupled, scalable, and faster to develop, deploy and debug. It is technology agnostic and has strong security.

But since the microservices architecture is standard across enterprise applications, there are often discussions on data lakehouse versus microservices. So let's start by explaining a few core components of the microservices architecture.

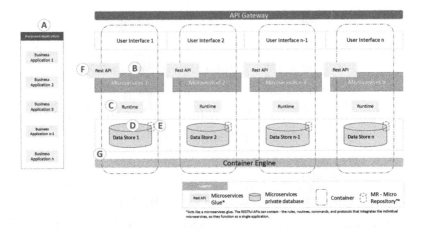

Figure 11-2. Data lakehouse architecture.Reference Microservices Architecture with a new Micro Repository™ concept

A. **Purposed application.** An enterprise can have multiple applications with similar workflows or functional requirements. Indeed, each independent service can't directly cater to each application's needs. But there is a way to handle it efficiently. And that is through micro-repository-based design. Within the microservices private database, we will have repositories that will help capture all the required properties for every individual but common application. Examples include applications that perform data pre-processing, data ingestion, data cleansing, data profiling, data standardization, data transformation, scheduling, reporting, BI, analytics, and visualization.

B. **Microservices.** To identify independent microservices in an application or group of applications requires end-to-end understanding and visibility of business needs. The purpose should be to identify independent services within the application that can help create loosely coupled services that work together to complete the purpose of the integrated application in a more efficient way than a monolithic architecture. Containerization and its management and orchestration can be an option for a seamless, integrated, and managed environment. Ensure a secure environment through API-security standards. Examples include microservices for the data lake, data warehouse, subject-oriented data marts, reporting microservices, advanced analytics microservices, and dashboards.

C. **Microservices runtime**. Microservices runtime is optimized for execution in a container. You can run a microservice or a set of related microservices in a container. A container image includes configuration, enabling you to deploy the same configuration anywhere.

D. **Microservices Private DB**. Each microservice can have a private database to persist the data required to implement the business functionality offered. A given microservice can only access the dedicated private database—not the databases of other microservices. For example, you might have to update several databases for a single transaction in some business scenarios. Do this through its service API only (and not through the database directly).

E. **Micro Repository™**. Micro Repository is a special purpose productization paradigm for creating multipurpose microservices. It helps use a common microservice to cater to more than one integrated application. The underlying repository consists of system references, parameters, rules, and commands/formulas that must be passed at runtime to fulfill different applications.

F. **Rest API.** You need to define and publish the service contract when implementing a business capability as a service. We need a capability that deals with REST as a first-class citizen. Since we build microservices on top of the REST architectural style, we can use the same REST API definition techniques to define the contract of the microservices. Therefore, microservices use the standard REST API definition languages, such as Swagger and RAML, to define the service contracts.

G. **Container and container engine**. An open-source container engine lets developers and system administrators deploy self-sufficient application containers in a given environment. Containers provide a great way to deploy microservices while addressing the requirements. First, package the microservice as a container image. Next, deploy each service instance as a container. Finally, scale it according to the number of container instances. Building, deploying, and starting a microservice will be much faster as we are using containers.

Micro Repository™

Remember that design patterns do not depend on a specific technology, framework, or programming language. A design pattern is a reusable solution to a general problem occurring in a given context in software design. A design pattern is not a design that is directly transferred into code.

A repository pattern separates the data access logic and maps it to the business entities in the business logic. Communication between the data access logic and the business logic occurs through interfaces.

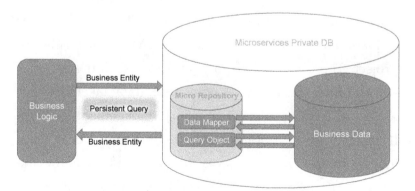

Figure 11-3. Data lakehouse architecture.A repository pattern is a kind of container where data access logic is stored.

It hides the details of data access logic from business logic. In other words, we allow business logic to access the data object without knowing the underlying data access architecture. The separation of data access from business logic has many benefits:

- Centralization of the data access logic makes code easier to maintain
- We can test business and data access logic separately
- Less duplication of code
- Lower chance for programming errors

In a nutshell, it is a technique to implement microservices within microservices.

Repository design patterns rely on interfaces. An interface acts like a contract that specifies what a concrete class must implement.

As an example, assume we have many ELT workflows for a National Airport Authority (NAA) data lakehouse project. There are 100 airports and the Airport Authority wants to create a central enterprise data lakehouse for eVPMS (Electronic Vehicle Parking Management System). It will cater to all user grievances related to overcharges or inappropriate charges. As a national authority of the airports of the nation, the airport authority in question wants the solution on a high priority basis.

Given facts:

- Authority – National Airport Authority
- Number of airports in scope – 100
- Five categories of airports (few volumetric):

Sr#	Category	No. of Airports	Vehicle entering airport
1	Category 1	1	20,000 / day
2	Category 2	9	10,000 / day
3	Category 3	10	5,000 / day
4	Category 4	15	3,000 / day
5	Category 5	65	1,000 / day

The source applications are in different states, like cloud, on-prem, standalone, or manual. So in any such scenario, we can have data objects from:

- Cloud sources – where concessionaire has an eVPMS hosted on cloud
- On premise sources – where the application is on premise
- Standalone sources – where the application is standalone
- Manual sources – where the system is still manual and/or the tickets issued are paper/slip based, and there is no direct machine involved

All sources are country-wide diversified airports sources.

Now, in such a case, we can think of a smart way of designing a microservice for the purpose where the same microservice can be overloaded. We can overload it through Micro Repository.

We understand here that whether the data comes from the cloud, on premise, standalone or a manual system, it gets ingested to the target staging of the data lake as part of the extract and load.

In this case, we may not need separate microservices for cloud sources, on premise sources, standalone sources, and manual sources. Rather we can leverage the power of the Micro Repository, where we can parameterize any such information that creates a multipurpose microservice.

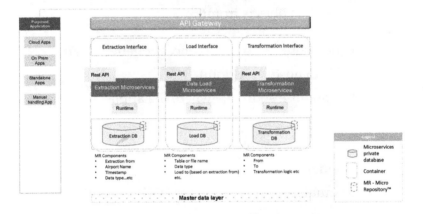

Figure 11-4. Data lakehouse architecture.Microservices-based Solution Architecture for ELT of eVPMS centralized data lakehouse as per this use case.

This diagram shows the reference architecture we discussed earlier that enables microservices multiuse using the Micro Repository.

So as you can see in the above solution diagram, no separate ingestion microservices are needed for different source data from diversified types of sources. Whether it is the extract microservices, load microservices, or transform microservices. Any such deviation in the variable parameters can use this new paradigm of the Micro Repository. We simply put a layer between the business logic and the microservices' databases called the micro repository layer.

Once you closely observe the overall implementation of the data lakehouse, you can understand why it is challenging to implement the microservices architecture end-to-end. Evaluate the impact of the microservices architecture for your data lakehouse project as to whether it benefits the enterprise goals by its successful implementation. There is no right or wrong answer. Such decisions are very situational and depend greatly on the nature of the business needs and the other parameters that vary from business to business.

Security

Security in the data lakehouse is important because of its nature of enterprise-wide implementations and capability of storing, preserving, and handling all types of data, including structured, semi-structured, and unstructured.

That means we are targeting to keep all kinds of enterprise data in the enterprise data lake underneath the lakehouse. Unfortunately, now it is more vulnerable to theft, cyber-attacks, and malware. Security at rest and security in motion are both important apart from network-level security, system-level security, database-level security, and application-level security. We suggest security at all levels:

- **Data security**. Including data security in motion and data security at rest
- **Application security**. Including secured application architecture, and standard and non-vulnerable coding practices
- **Hardware security**. Including device, equipment level, network, and communications level security
- **Physical security**. Including tailgating prohibition, accompanied guest, and CCTV surveillance
- **Business security**. Including business policy for security, tailgate policy, and mandatory escorting rules for visitors
- **Organizational guidelines**

Index

acquisition, 96, 98

acronym, 40

analog/IoT, 1, 4, 5, 6, 62, 83

ATM, 3, 17, 18

canonical data model, 61, 62, 63, 67, 68

CCPA, 106

connector, 55, 56, 64, 65

COPPA, 106

correlation, 52, 59

data confidentiality, 105

data extraction, 98, 99, 100

data future-proofing, 110

data governance, 124

data integration, 98

data interoperability, 98

data lake, 2, 7, 8, 9, 10, 72, 74, 83, 85, 87, 89, 96, 97, 99, 100, 101, 106, 107, 111, 119, 130, 139, 140, 143, 145, 150, 152

data lakehouse, i, ii, iii, 2, 3, 6, 7, 8, 9, 10, 11, 61, 62, 63, 71, 72, 73, 74, 75, 77, 78, 79, 80, 81, 83, 85, 86, 87, 88, 89, 96, 97, 98, 99, 100, 101, 102, 103, 105, 106, 107, 108, 111, 119, 120, 122, 123, 124, 125, 127, 128, 129, 130, 131, 139, 140, 141, 142, 143,148, 150, 151

data lakehouse housekeeping, 97, 124, 125

data privacy, 104, 105, 107

data protection, 106

data science, 102

data security, 104

data swamp, 2, 96, 139

data transformation, 98, 100

data warehouse, i, ii, 1, 26, 27, 28, 29, 30, 69, 70, 71, 73, 74, 75, 78, 83, 84, 85, 86, 87, 89, 91, 92, 96, 101, 111, 130, 139, 140, 143, 145

dimensional modeling, 28, 130

ETL. See Extract, Transform, and Load

Extract, Transform, and Load, 28, 70

FDM. See Future-proof Data Management, See Future-proof Data Management

FERPA, 106

Future-proof Data Management, 89, 122, 123, 127, 128

GDPR, 106

GLBA, 106

governance, 89, 91, 96

hasher, 16

heuristic analysis, 54

HIPAA, 106

homographic resolution, 35

index, 15, 16, 90

inline contextualization, 36

IoT, 98

Key Performance Indicator, 74, 91

KPI. See Key Performance Indicator

master reference, 97, 101, 102, 103

medical records, 111

microservice, 145, 146, 149, 150

Natural Language Processing, 91

negation, 40

NLP. See Natural Language Processing

OCR. See Optical Character Recognition

OLAP, 130, 131

Optical Character Recognition, 88

primary key, 16

randomizer, 16

RDBMS. See Relational Database Management Systems

Relational Database Management Systems, 31

repository pattern, 147

routine maintenance lifecycle, 125

SDLC. See Software Development Lifecycle

sentiment analysis, 39

service level agreement, 18

single version of the truth, 26, 70, 97, 102, 104

SLA. See service level agreement

Social Security Number, 14, 15, 35, 39, 56, 112, 117

Software Development Lifecycle, 24

spider web environment, 1

star join, 28

structured environment, 4, 5, 6, 13, 62

surveillance, 5, 45, 46, 62, 152

taxonomical resolution, 37

textual disambiguation, 34, 37, 41

textual environment, 4, 5, 6, 62

textual ETL, 1, 37, 78, 91, 100

visualization, 42, 132, 144

warranty, 2

www.ingramcontent.com/pod-product-compliance
Lightning Source LLC
Chambersburg PA
CBHW071250050326
40690CB00011B/2328

9 781634 622783